How to Become President

A Practical Handbook

Felix Petitzon

Contents

Preface

This book is a practical guide. It explains stratagems, techniques, and manipulations employed by past victorious candidates which can lead you to the presidency. It also goes over pitfalls and traps that destroyed political careers, which you need to avoid. You should compare it to a cookbook. A person with a strong desire can become president by following the rights instructions, just as one can succeed at baking a cake.

Set ambitious goals, strive hard, and you will realize your full potential. This is what self-improvement books such as the bestseller 'Think and Grow Rich' from Napoleon Hill declare. Therein the author moans all book long that you have to desire riches really hard, and work really really hard at it, and hopes this will somehow inspire you. Although this is as a general observation of course true, such truisms are not very helpful. In this work, I set forth concrete and usable strategies instead. I will not dwell on philosophical and theoretical contemplation but concentrate on practical advice.

The focus lies on how to strive for and attain the highest position in a democratic state with universal suffrage. In the following pages, I do not preoccupy myself with other ways of seizing powers such as coup d'états or power struggles within dictatorships or monarchies. There are already sufficient good on those topics ('Coup d'État', from E. Luttwak, or 'The Prince' from N. Machiavelli).

This book will also not bother with nations where the head of state has few powers and merely serves in a protocol role.

Examples in modern times are Italy or Germany, whose current presidents are unknown even by their own citizens. These persons serve nowadays in a ceremonial role, although numerous strategies can be gleaned from the history of both countries. I will study the United States, France, Brazil, Taiwan, South-Korea, countries from Latin America, and all the other states where the president is elected by the people and holds substantial sway. Much of the content of this handbook could also help aspiring prime ministers in countries with parliamentary systems.

The office of president, which entails significant influence, control, and prestige, is the highest position a citizen can gain. Surprisingly enough, no books or guides have been written on the matter. The president's role combines the head of state, the head of the government, and the head of the armed forces. Undoubtedly, many readers have contemplated taking up themselves this role and leading their country. One is thrilled when watching the news and see the impact a president produces on his or her country.

This manual will help you achieve the highest office. It is for the enthusiastic and determined persons who wish to change their country for the better and desire making history. If this endeavor might seem too ambitious and beyond your capabilities, then keep in mind that all those precedent presidents were but mere mortals. Few wrote their speeches. And they often stole credit from other's labor. The only reason they were in charge is that they knew what they wanted and dared to strive for it.

Anyone with the right attitude, who aspires to become president—including you—, can use this book as a blueprint to achieve this. Rigorous study of past and recent elections shows that all successful presidential candidates have undertaken the same steps described within this work. Armed with the knowledge contained in this guide, you too can attain the presidency and reap its rewards.

When striving for the highest power, you will inevitably alienate some persons. Adversaries and rivals will be numerous. This is natural and no reason for concern. As Clemenceau said, ''Never worry about making enemies; if you have no enemies, you are a nobody.'' Don't fear other contenders. Let them lose sleep over you, not the reverse.

Felix Petitzon

Zürich, December 2019

Chapter 1
Introduction

You can sway a thousand men
by appealing to their prejudices
quicker than you can convince one man by logic
— Robert Heinlein

Before turning to the practical advice in the next chapters, some general theory is useful. This serves as a classification of methods, to structure our analysis of presidential campaigns thereafter.

Logos, Ethos, and Pathos

Already in ancient Greek times, a variety of orators and philosophers studied the art of persuasion. In the 5th century BC, Athens was a growing democracy where oratory skills were in high demand. A new profession emerged at the time: sophist. A sophist made a living educating young men from wealthy families in the art of rhetoric. Rhetorical techniques were valuable for any young nobleman looking for public office in the flourishing city. The sophists would also participate in debates, speeches, and act as lawyers at trials. To showcase their skills, they organized mock debates. Therein, they would defend one point, but next—to the public's joy—switch side. They proceeded then to attack the same position they minutes ago had defended with so much apparent sincerity.

What words would entertain, impress, or persuade an audience? When debating and trying to convince people, the ancient Athenians discovered different types of arguments. Not much has changed to the fundamental human nature and the psychology of masses since those times. The ancient Greek philosopher Aristotle already made the following classification of the means of persuasions. There are arguments based on facts and reasons (**Logos**), arguments based on character (**Ethos**), and arguments based on emotion (**Pathos**).

Logos (from which the word logic is derived), for example, is a careful cost-benefit analysis. Or an advanced statistical analysis of historical data used to discover empirical facts. Or it could be a logically structured reasoning: A implies B, B implies C; therefore, A implies C. The idea of this mode of persuasion is that the arguments advanced prove the truth.

Ethos encompasses persuasion techniques linked to the morality, credibility, or competence of specific individuals. This could be an appeal to authoritative persons to prove your point. For instance, you could say an economic program is excellent because a Nobel Prize laureate in Economics supports it. Or others could endorse your skills and experience. Or you could decry the shady and untrustworthy character of your opponents and attempt to discredit him or her in this fashion.

Pathos employs the inherent instincts and sentiments of humankind. A well-told 'true story' can evoke sympathy or compassion from the audience. And fear, rage, and hope can all be stirred to sway the public to your cause. Moreover, such emotion-based arguments can circulate like viruses, as people spread the word.

When debating with friends or in small groups (at home, at work, at the university), you should wield a mix of all three classes of arguments. Logos, ethos, and pathos have roughly equal strength in such discussions. In this context, an astute person will blend all three methods of persuasion in his or her speech. But small groups of acquaintances and peers are not representative of interactions in a democratic nation.

Logos is weak when campaigning

In elections, arguments based on pathos, and to some extend ethos, are the most potent.

Why does logos play such a small part in elections? Firstly, it takes time to assess the merits of a proposal. Voters simply don't have much time to analyze all candidates' proposals in detail. They don't have a lot of information, and so they substitute a reasoned examination with a quick judgment based on their intuitive, emotional feeling (pathos). Additionally, a voter will seek guidance from authoritative persons he or she trusts (ethos), and will superficially appraise a candidate's character (ethos), to decide for whom to vote.

Furthermore, modern states contain millions of voters from various backgrounds and with different interests. Individuals and small groups don't behave like crowds at mass rallies. The behavior of the masses is a whole new field compared to the psychology of the individual. This difference is true not only in elections but also in demonstrations or in sports matches where tens of thousands of supporters gather. In front of a crowd, logical arguments lose strength compared to appeals to feelings. Pathos is, in particular, strong when addressing crowds because emotions are contagious. Hence the behavior of the mass favors pathos over logos; adapt your expression and speech in consequence.

Another ground why arguments based on reason are weak is that voters don't value their material self-interest when voting. A large number of studies on this topic have shown this. For example, even many affluent voters support candidates that pledge higher taxes. And vice versa, many poor vote for candidates wishing to lower taxes. This is especially valid for countrywide elections. In municipal elections, self-interest prevails on a much larger scale than in a presidential election. In ballots with a large number of voters, however, most persons vote with their guts. Logical and proven plans to improve the situation, whatever their merits, hold little weight. Ideas and emotions dominate instead.

This is not as illogical as may seem at first sight. A single vote in a presidential election never matters. Even in the 'closest' calls—such Bush vs. Gore in Florida, which generated massive controversy at the time—the winner had a margin of more than three hundred votes (and more after oversea ballots were counted). In El Salvador, Sánchez Cerén (50.11%) won the 2014 presidential election in a neck-to-neck race versus Norman Quijano (49.89%). But since the country consists of nearly 3 million voters, this narrow percentage lead was, in reality, more than 6,000 votes.

No individual, family, or village voting differently would have been of consequence. The probability that a single ballot flips the election, even in smaller countries, is nil. Why should then a citizen vote for his or her own benefit? Or why would a citizen bother researching the best ways to improve the nation's wealth? This would cost such a person a lot of time and energy, yet his or her single vote would not alter the election result. It is easier to stay at home and spend time with friends or family, or exert hobbies, rather than try defeating statistical odds. Therefore, there is for a voter no incentive to inform oneself.

Why does a citizen go to the booth in the polling station at all? It is not because a single vote matters, but because it provides psychological gratification. It is pleasing to cheer on to a team (in football or politics). It is also pleasing to punish those we don't like. A citizen can feel satisfied after casting the ballot, though their individual action did not affect the outcome of the race. Voting is an expressive statement. This requires no significant effort from a voter, nor is a voter rewarded for spending much time investigating the right choice for the country.

With this in mind, your objective is to make them feel good. The details of the implementation of your program are not crucial. But say the right emotional platitudes to appeal to how they feel, and you will win their affection. The population will cast a vote to make a statement, not to produce good policy. That is why those that best employ pathos stand the largest chances in a presidential election. You must understand and capitalize on the passions of the electorate to defeat your opponents. Political campaigns are hence done with poetry, not with prose.

Ethos matters for presidential elections

Arguments based on ethos, such as endorsement from celebrities or politicians, are also crucial. This is above all true in presidential systems, where people vote for a person foremost instead of for a party list.

In parliamentary systems, the party leader has less impact on the election's outcome (smaller leader effect). The reasons are twofold.

Firstly, people vote for a party, or a member of a party, and not directly for the head of state or head of government. For illustration, Theresa May became British Prime Minister in 2016, even though she had not led the British Conservatives in the previous election. (David Cameron led the party in the 2015 election.) Voters know this and hence pay more attention to the overall party program, rather than its leader, which could change even without new elections

Secondly, the prime minister remains dependent on his or her party's support. Continuing the previous British case, Theresa May faced significant opposition from her own party in 2019. Her proposed Brexit deal failed multiple times to pass, because members of her party rejected it. In July 2019, she resigned and her internal rival, Boris Johnson, was appointed as Prime Minister instead. May could not act independently from her party, and, in the end, the Conservative Party prevailed over the individual.

In contrast, presidents, once in power, can act independently of the party. They can carry out the administration of the executive branch without needing to ask for approval. And they can veto laws, even when those laws are supported by their own party. Take, for example, the case of the Water Resources Development Act of 2007 that US President G.W. Bush opposed even though it had large bipartisan support. That law mandated the use of the US Army to improve waterways, and funded projects to protect ecosystems. President Bush went against his own party—without fear—and vetoed the law on grounds that it did not set priorities and lacked fiscal discipline. A prime minister would not get away with such behavior.

That is why in presidential elections the position of the party on a topic matters less than the intrinsic qualities of a single person, since the president can act so freely. All this turns presidential elections into highly personalized competitions. The press and the voters will emphasize a candidate's character and aptitude at leading the nation (ethos). But even his or her looks, family, or other personal traits will be scrutinized.

*

In the next chapters, I set out actionable strategies and techniques. I will explain how to develop a plan to win the mandate of the people. With the strength of pathos and ethos in mind, the book is structured in four parts. You will learn in

Part I - what issues your political program should address, to satisfy the passions of the people;

Part II - how to style your communication to get your message across, by employing modern technology and advertising techniques;

Part III - how to adapt to the political landscape;

Part IV - how to convince voters of your upright character.

Part I -
Pick the right message

Chapter 2
Support popular policies

A billion here, a billion there,
and soon we are talking real money
— senator Everett Dirksen

The electorate is divided into three parts: left-wing, right-wing, and center. By definition, the last regroup persons with moderate, middle of the road views. You might hold a personal political preference, yet it is better if you don't. That way, instead of remaining stubborn, you can adapt your declared convictions to the situation at hand.

As the three parts of the political spectrum tend to be of roughly equal size, each gives you an equally good starting position. As long as you are not too far from the center of the political landscape, you will be able to build up a strong and credible program. Regardless of your political orientation, you will need to set forth new ambitious policy proposals.

As outlined in the introduction, voters have no incentive to investigate the details of your proposals. To a large extent, the electorate is uninformed. They are not able to analyze your comprehensive plans and their impact on the nation's welfare. Therefore, you need to provide a simple message that the broad masses will understand, and that appeals to their sentiments. For—remember—elections are won through pathos and not through logos. So, how to determine the content of your campaign? Follow the instructions within this and the next chapters.

Promise a lot

As long as you are not in power, make many promises. If you break a pledge after you are elected, the outcome is uncertain. People might have forgotten, circumstances changed, and you are anyway president then. But if you refuse to make promises during the electoral campaign, the effect is immediate—you will lose potential voters. The downside to promising is limited, but the upside large. Hence promise a lot.

Why wouldn't you? People love it when politicians pledge to lower taxes, bring peace, provide better healthcare, improve education, etcetera. Include many good sounding promises and proposals into your core message to the electorate. Helping the poor, the old, all will have more income; you will sound generous. Don't hold back. In reality, you are spending taxpayer money, and not a single cent will come out of your pocket anyway (quite the contrary). As Machiavelli wrote more than 500 years ago: ''Spending the wealth of others does not lessen your reputation, but adds to it.''

Part of the population will believe your promises because they think they will gain from it, another part because they are not very smart, and yet another part because hope dies last. Next, I will detail how you can optimize your promises; you shouldn't do such things haphazardly.

What to promise

As a politician, you will only succeed insofar your political program aligns with the general opinion of the electorate. If you, in contrast, antagonize public opinion, you are doomed to failure.

An intelligent candidate must give the people what they wish, just like successful businesses provide customers what they want.

Concretely, when deciding what policy to favor, or wish side to choose on a contentious issue, follow the polls. Favor what public opinion favors and oppose whatever is unpopular. In a democracy, following the majority is a simple and effective way to gain voters. Vice versa, taking unpopular stances won't gain you sympathy. Also, tackle in your program the top issues on people's minds, and not side topics that don't interest the electorate.

By following polls, you will be able to measure the inclination of your fellow countrymen. Polls are lagging, which means they give you info that is 1-2 weeks outdated. It takes time to interview and process the data. For most issues, though, the public opinion won't change that fast for it to matter.

Why follow polls and not a more sophisticated and complex methodology? Because understanding humans is hard. They are complicated, it is never clear why they believe certain things, and there are so many of them. Some politicians think they can influence the electorate's position by the mere force of their logical arguments. This is quite naive since pathos, not logos, dominates elections.

No one quite knows why the mood of the public swings in one or the other way. Predicting it is close to impossible; humans are not electrons. There are always those individuals who—believing they are more gifted than the large part of humankind—wish to appear wiser than the majority. Out of a desire to prove their moral and intellectual superiority, they lecture the voters on what is right and wrong. They never win elections. Maybe such an approach functions in the arts, science, technology, or whatever, but in the realm of politics, it is suicide.

People have preconceived biases; they have already made up their minds and they won't deviate. On fresh topics, the public might not have a strong opinion yet and is malleable. A persuasive speech, delivered by a person the people respect (ethos), which appeals to their sentiments (pathos), can shape the opinion. It remains nevertheless risky. On a prominent and much-discussed topic—let's say the Iraq War in the US 2008 election—, each individual already has its opinion set in stone. Maneuvering contrary to the passion of people is then like paddling upstream in a mountain torrent. Don't even try going against the prevailing mood.

Therefore, as a general rule, favor what voters like, oppose what they dislike, promise them what they want. Don't swim against the tide. The best way to discover what the electorate wants is by polling them. Question a bunch of voters, tally their answers, and draw your conclusions. Ensure the sample of the survey is statistically representative of the whole electorate likely to go vote. In case it is not, apply statistical methods to remove any bias in the sample. Sophisticated large political parties should already have teams doing this 365 days a year and all around the clock.

Angela Merkel, four times Chancellor of the German Federal Republic, orders regular surveys on a wide variety of topics. She can that way monitor the inclination of the German people and detect early new trends. Her 'flip-flops' on multiple subjects have followed the shift in the public's opinion.

One notorious case was the topic of nuclear power plants, which she used to vigorously defend against all criticism. On 11 March 2011, the Fukushima nuclear disaster occurred. This high profile event caused alarm in Germany, which had numerous nuclear reactors. Within weeks, Merkel announced that all of Germany's nuclear power plants would close by 2022. Eight out of the seventeen operating reactors in Germany were already permanently shut down by August 2011. Merkel's rapid and energetic pivot was unexpected by her opponents, but she so maintained high approval rates. She would go on to her largest victory in the next election. Such shrewdness and timely turnarounds are required to gain and remain in power.

It is worth repeating here—I know some of my readers will discard this advice because they think it is too ordinary: You should poll the people and position yourself in line with their views. If their favorite color is yellow, your favorite color is yellow too.

In the 2016 US Republican primary, the eventual winner Donald Trump was most known for his eccentric manner and brash statements. Despite this, Trump was on substance the most moderate of all Republican candidates. Other contenders, for example, firmly opposed the Affordable Care Act (ACA, also known as Obamacare). Trump instead often took a softer stance and announced he would not gut Obamacare.

At the time, polls showed that many aspects of the Act were popular with Americans. The creation of health insurance exchanges, allowing young adults to remain on their parents' insurance until age 26, and protections for preexisting conditions were all well-liked. That is why an intelligent and ruthless leader like Trump declared in the primary: ''I'm not going to cut Social Security like every other Republican and I'm not going to cut Medicare or Medicaid.'' Trump's opponents' ideological opposition to Obamacare clouded their judgment. By opposing popular measures, they lost votes. The only part of the ACA that was unpopular was the individual mandate—the requirement that many people who don't have health insurance pay a fine. Always remember that the population doesn't like taxes and fines. Trump had it abolished shortly after he came to power; he maintained the other popular provisions.

Another historical case is from Charles de Gaulle in 1958. These were tumultuous times for the French Fourth Republic. In those days, Algeria was part of France. Millions of French colonists lived, and hundreds of thousands of soldiers were stationed there. The at that time ongoing Algerian War caused significant friction within society. The situation deteriorated so far that the French Army openly plotted a coup to overthrow the government. Sensing the danger, the French Parliament dismissed the executive. Former general Charles de Gaulle was next appointed to head of the new government. De Gaulle benefited from an aura of dignity and authority dating back to the Second World War, grounded in his command of the Free French against the Nazis. He was also a great orator and delivered speeches that marked French history.

Upon becoming head of the new government, he raced to Algeria. He acquired a good read on the mood of the people. He next gave a speech to the assembled crowd in Alger, stating, ''Je vous ai compris!'' (I have understood you!) This soothed the civilians and the soldiers present; they now felt reassured that this new government would not abandon them. De Gaulle would be their voice; he would defend them from the untrustworthy politicians in Paris. De Gaulle, this way, calmed the rebellious elements in France, and so a coup was avoided. Having strengthened his position by taking popular stances, de Gaulle returned to Paris. There he imposed his terms and wrested power from the French Parliament: he turned France into a presidential system and became president shortly after that.

The key phrase from his speech in Algeria itself was ambiguous, though. Yet each group left satisfied in the belief de Gaulle had vowed support. A few years later, the Algerian War was still unresolved. It became increasingly unpopular because of the cost the war imposed and because of the year-long deployment of conscripts. The tide was turning against the martial ideology hitherto prevalent. The revelation that the French armed forces had used torture caused significant concern among the electorate. The memory of the Gestapo (the secret police of Nazi Germany) and their methods was namely still fresh. De Gaulle, sensing the change of wind, departed from his previous views. He now supported negotiation with the Algerians and granting them independence. In January 1961, he held a referendum, and the French backed him with 75% supporting the peace talks. In this manner, de Gaulle remained beloved and the French re-elected him later on.

De Gaulle succeeded because he picked the right message at the right time, and adapted when necessary. And so, he became France's greatest president.

Drifts in opinion

People's opinions in politics drift over time. This is because of aging and discussions with their friends and acquaintances. While transformation of the opinion of the electorate is often slow, there are circumstances where support for a policy or principle can explode. The mechanism causing this rapid change goes as follows: (1) The social pressure of family, colleagues, and society constrains people's convictions. The few that hold unpopular views will remain silent in public out of fear being ostracized. (2) But over time or through events, the minority can grow into the silent majority. Most won't even realize how numerous they have become or how popular an opinion is until some braves share their thoughts. (3) People will be surprised that so many support a presumed disfavored view. Yet the more persons talk about it, the more it will gain acceptance. There is safety in numbers. Those that had remained reticent to voice their opinion won't fear expressing their view now. And also many individuals are like sheep; they will adjust their opinions and follow whatever they believe their neighbor believes.

This process can cause sudden shifts in beliefs; this happened time again throughout history.

Homosexuality was taboo and, in some countries, criminalized during most of the 20th century. People considered it unnatural and disgusting. Then in the 1990s, within a decade, the public's opinion evolved on the matter. As more individuals came out, more felt empowered to express their sexual orientation. Films would feature a homosexual, or people would have an acquaintance from the LGTB community. And so the population became accustomed to homosexuality. Support for additional rights climbed at the beginning of the 21st century. In 2001, front-runner Netherlands legalized same-sex marriage. As of today, support for it has soared in Northern America, Western Europe, and in most Latin America. You better not express yourself against it if you wish to become president; there is nowadays no majority to roll this back. The majority swung from disgust to strong support in a mere 2-3 election cycles in those countries.

The above is an illustration of the rapid fluctuation in the mood of the electorate. Yet there are many more dramatic examples. The fall of communism in Eastern Europe happened in the span of a few months, for example. Despite that many opposed the regime, the Communist Party had remained for decades in power. The reason is that, although many opposed the system, each individual assumed that others were supporters of it. Therefore, the majority were afraid to voice their opposition because they feared being a minority.

A more recent event occurred at the end of 2010, when Ben Ali ruled Tunisia. His strong and stable leadership had guided the country for 23 years. One day, some fruit-seller was bullied by the local administration and beaten by the police. The humiliated fruit-seller set himself on fire as a protest against his rough and unfair treatment. This self-immolation caused some first, timid protest in Tunisia. As images spread across social media, more individuals voiced their dislike of the corrupt regime. Massive demonstrations erupted, once the people realized how unpopular Ben Ali was. The dissenters gained confidence when the protests swelled, for there is safety in numbers. When a hundred men participate, the protesters have a problem. Conversely, when a million join, the government has a problem. Previously, the people had not opposed Ben Ali, out of conformism, fear of retaliation, and inertia. But within weeks, a majority opposing

Ben Ali emerged. The dictatorship was brought down, and Ben Ali fled the country. The successful revolution in Tunisia encouraged protests in other Arab countries as well. The death of a single person in this way sparked the entire Arab Spring. This resulted in massive protests across the Middle East and the fall of dictators. No one—not even the best intelligence agencies—saw it coming.

It is hard to predict what people will like or hate next. You have to figure out where the big waves are and adjust your course.

Don't be too ideological. François Mitterrand, after multiple narrow defeats in previous elections, finally became President of France in 1981. He did so on a left-wing populist platform. Two years in his presidency, his political agenda wasn't working, so he changed course. This was called 'the turn towards rigor.' His face-turn disappointed his allies but secured continued economic prosperity and hence his re-election.

Trump, in private, often admitted that he had no strong feelings on many topics. In the past, he had a socially liberal inclination and had supported Democrats. Donald Trump is no convinced conservative. But he smartly surfed the anti-immigration wave. And he also caught the growing anti-Chinese feeling. China's ascend turned it into an economic and military rival of the United States. Its rising power challenges American supremacy. The totalitarian Communist Party that rules China is now a contestant of the American world order. Donald Trump branded China as an antagonist at the right time, not too early, not too late. Aspiring to seize (democratic) control of the country, you should emulate him in this regard. Adjust the content of your campaign to the prevailing mood and the latest fashionable trends in the country. Some ideological flexibility is required; otherwise, you end up hammering your head against the wall.

Adapt as well to the subset of citizens in the election. Mitt Romney was the Republican candidate for the US presidential election in 2012. He repeatedly spoke out in favor of abortion when running in the US state of Massachusetts gubernatorial elections. This is natural, as the population from Massachusetts is very liberal. Romney wouldn't have won the gubernatorial race and become governor otherwise.

During the GOP primaries, he later changed his mind and spoke out against it. He modified his opinions depending on the ballot he stood on. This was wise because the Republican primary consists of a different electorate than back home in Massachusetts. The voters rewarded Mitt Romney for altering his message, and he ended up securing the Republican nomination for the presidential election.

Taxes and free stuff

Two imperatives are best kept in mind when you start determining your campaign content and promises. The first rule you need to remember: you will always vow to lower taxes for the broad base of the population. You don't have to fulfill that pledge thereafter, yet it is needed in the first place to win the race. Bill Clinton, two times US President, walked away from his vow to cut income taxes—but only after being elected. George H.W. Bush, US President from 1989 till 1993, also pledged no tax increases. The most famous phrase from his campaign was: ''Read my lips: no new taxes.'' When campaigning, it is bon ton to complain about the taxes that crush the middle and lower classes. People don't like taxes unless it targets a small minority to which they don't belong. If the tax burden is in disproportion carried by a small subset of the population, the people will support you. Such well-aimed taxes have been used by a multitude of candidates to win elections. Taxing the ultra-rich, or the bankers, or a poll tax in the racist South of the USA, or a special tax on and redistribution of land in South Africa to target white farmers (Boers) are but a few examples.

The second imperative is: do not charge for something that was provided for free in the past. Assure voters they will receive free goods or services. As marketing departments discovered already long ago, free items cause the human brain to short-circuit. If you sell a product and enact a drastic cut in the price, your sales will increase. Whereas, if you declare it free, the sales will explode. Somehow, the transition from cheap to free is a crucial step in the subconscious of consumers. This goes both ways: pricing a product that was until then free will cause uproar and a radical change in behavior. In the United Kingdom, the sales of plastic bags plummeted 90% after the price jumped from 0 pence to a puny 5 pence, for example. For that reason, it is a blunder to talk about charging for previously costless services. The people's subconscious, emotional selves would detest you and would dismiss any rational argument you would advance.

How realistic your promises should be

The ambitious agenda you set forth should be a little unrealistic. Campaigning for president is, after all, not done with logic but with emotion, as seen in Chapter I. You have to sell them a dream;

you must show them you have a project for the nation. No one will vote for a passive president. They want someone that has bold plans, someone who dares. They crave for a true leader. Why else would you run for president if it was only to defend the status quo?

You won't be an idle president; you will need to convince your voters of that fact. Although some of your plans will be impractical, this will not hurt your reputation as long as your proposals are well-liked by the population. It will instead signal that you are not a cynical person. Prove the population you are willing to pursue your ideals by creating an unrealistic political program. Your message should contain your goals, your values, and your generous promises. Don't detail too much *how* you will achieve those goals; focus instead on *what* your political manifesto contains.

How to finance your promises

Who will pay for all your promises? At some point, pundits will question your agenda. When it comes to the costs of your plans, spend great care. Loudly promising to 55% of the electorate that you will redistribute money from the other 45% doesn't work. The 45% percent will realize you are acting against them and vehemently oppose you. Yet the 55% won't be grateful enough because, after all, the spoils are spread out so widely that the benefits will be marginal. How should you then finance your promises? When promising stuff that requires money, follow one of the three successful approaches detailed next.

1) concentrated benefits, diluted costs

The first method is to promise a lot to a small group in the hope the larger part of the population doesn't care or doesn't notice. This group deserves help through direct political action. This 'concentrated benefits, diluted costs' is effective for two reasons. The small group you showered with subsidies, tax savings, spending, or jobs will be devoted to your cause. And the vast majority will not notice or care, though, because the cost will be dispersed over the whole nation. It will therefore only amount to a small burden per person.

A proper political move, for example, is to pledge extra subsidies to farmers. Although farmers represent only 2-3% of the population in western nations, they are organized in active lobby groups that exert significant political pressure. They will block-vote for the person guaranteeing the highest subsidies. Sugar subsidies in the USA, for instance, cost all Americans roughly $50 per year. (On average, US sugar prices are approximately twice as high as world prices.) As $50 isn't so noticeable, many citizens shrug it off or remain ignorant. In the mean-time, this $50 from 300 million indifferent Americans gets funneled into the pockets of the small number of farmers. These accordingly pay a lot of attention to this topic, unlike the rest.

But you wouldn't formulate it like this if someone challenges you on this topic. You should instead answer by expressing concern about the current plight affecting farmers, especially the small farmers. The public will either feel compassion, or think you have it, and won't feel threatened because you will downplay the actual sums of money.

The notorious pork barrel metaphor, whereby government spending is used for very localized projects, is another instance of the 'concentrated benefits, diluted cost' approach. This type of project's sole purpose is to bring money to a small geographic area. This could be because it is a swing district in a presidential election, or it could be done to secure the (re-)election of a representative or member of parliament.

The key to success is not to extend such promises too blatantly. Provide such commitments in a rather closed environment in front of the appropriate audiences. Sponsor the policies that serve that particular group. To the farmer association, pledge agricultural subsidies; and to the local community, promise a bridge; and when speaking to teachers, reassure them of whatever they want; and cycle through any such groups, and promise them their heart's desire. Bait each association in turn, so that each feels special and privileged. You will show them generosity and consideration. Each group will believe you are at their side because you will entice them with the idea they can live at the expense of all others.

2) Conceal the costs

The second strategy is to promise benefits but obfuscate the costs. The public will only see the upside, but not the downside and therefore cheer you on. How can one obfuscate expenses? There are multiple existing ways, although this should not hold you back from inventing new financial tricks to achieve this.

The most classic, straightforward move is to finance it through a budget deficit. Having the state borrow money kicks the can down the road, as interests and, eventually, the principal will need to be repaid. But this is in the far future, a problem for those who will come long after your two terms. This is not only convenient for you, yet the public itself won't care. The benefit of your promise will immediately be realized. It is unclear who, in the long-term, foots the bill. The debt you will add to the government is much less visible than a tax hike. Which group will pay the interests? None feel like they are losing out or are attacked by your promise. Such debt spending is widespread, and it bears no surprise that near all democracies are heavily indebted.

3) Tax the people over there

The third approach to promising costly but well-loved programs is to assure the burden will be carried by a small subset of the population. In a later chapter, I explain how to pick that minority and write in detail about the usefulness that handful on which you shall concentrate the blame. Exploit them to finance your promises. This minority serves as a punching bag and should never be kept far because they provide convenient campaign material. Whether new projects, increased social spending, or tax cuts—the cost will be carried by the handful unlucky which you have chosen to attack. The majority will revel at this.

The French President François Hollande, for instance, came to power by campaigning on ''Mon Enemy, c'est la Finance'' (Finance is my enemy). And Hollande also signaled his intent to implement a 75% income tax rate on revenue earned above 1 million euros per year. The funds would be used to develop suburbs and to return to a deficit of zero percent of GDP. It was a popular act, since the majority of the French hoped to gain a share of the pie at the expense of the despised bankers and CEOs.

Promising applied

Let's look at more historical cases to illustrate these three approaches.

In the 1860 electoral campaign, Abraham Lincoln's posters read: "Vote Yourself a Farm." He thereby promised colonists land in the western parts of the United States. After expelling the Native Americans, the USA namely conquered a lot of land in the West. These so-called 'federal territories' were not yet part of any state; the US federal government, led by the President, administered them. Many on the East Coast were poor European farmers that had emigrated to the US. Those wishing to migrate West, build a farm, and flourish hoped for Lincoln's victory.

This is an example of the **first approach** since a few colonists would benefit from this policy and hence favored Lincoln. The others didn't care so much that a president would give away federal land as there was so much of it. The empty stretches in the West were anyway without value unless people turned them to productive use.

Furthermore, in some sense, the Natives were a targeted minority. The Indigenous Americans had no voting rights and served as a punching bag for several successful political careers in the earlier centuries. The theft of their lands and free distributions to colonists could, therefore, as well be classified as part of the third strategy.

One group you should particularly pay consideration to—as part of the first strategy—are the elderly. Announce they should be helped by direct political action. Barack Obama, in his electoral campaign, was well aware of this. "I will eliminate all income taxation of seniors making less than $50,000 per year. […] This will also mean that 27 million seniors will not need to file an income tax return at all,'' he promised.

Why are they so important and deserve so much attention? You can't disregard the retired voters because they have a high turnout in elections. They have nothing to do all day, and going out to vote is for them a social excursion and an excellent way to kill time. That is why they form a disproportionate share of the voters in comparison to the overall adult population. Your objective is to convince the people who go vote, i.e., the actual electorate. Don't waste time, money, or effort on those who have voting rights but are unlikely to go vote.

It is, therefore, vital to promise a lot to the politically attentive slice of the population, such as the elderly. Pledge lower taxes for them, guarantee increasing public pensions, and defend inter-generational solidarity. Resort to more traditional channels of communication (television, physical mail) that the youth eschew to pass on this message.

In the 2019 Polish election, the Law and Justice Party won by promising something to every group. The youth would be exempted from income tax, parents would receive extra child benefits, and the pension age would be lowered. Hence every age band felt they got cake. Depending on the communication channel, they highlighted different parts of their program to whet the appetite of the audience. Each age category appreciated that the Law and Justice Party would enrich them at the expense of everyone else. The party's lavish promises led them once more to victory.

In recent times in the USA, student debt has been a prominent topic in political discourse. Notable politicians have called for canceling the outstanding student debt. While this is an example of the first strategy that appeals to students and recently graduated, this approach is dubious for two reasons. The youth anyway has a lower voter turnout. And the part of the population that did pay off their student debt will furthermore resent such policy, as it financially disadvantages them. In addition, they will experience such a promise as unfair and perceive it as a slap in their face.

Offending people's dignity is worse than taking their money, so don't do it. Important is not only that your proposed policy financially aids a group, but you should also express a lot of sympathy for them. The content of your campaign should never slight the pride of a large group of the population. Because, often, dignity is more important than money. A group of voters might reward you for some promise that doesn't lead to a lot of financial gain for them but restores their pride and self-esteem. On the flip side, voters will punish you more for belittling them than for any financial loss. For illustration, Mexicans legally residing within the US have not suffered negative consequences from Donald J. Trump's victory. Yet they dislike him because Trump so often held derogatory speeches about them.

Imposing tariffs on trade is an illustration of the **second approach**. Most consumers don't directly see the impact of this tax, or they believe foreigners pay it. In reality, it disfavors companies that import or export a lot. All the people who have a stake in such businesses, as employees, suppliers, or shareholders, pay the cost indirectly. Consumers will also face reduced choice or higher prices as the tariffs are passed through to them.

Nevertheless, this is not so visible, and considerable doubt will exist on whom the incidence of the tax lays, which is why it is an effective approach.

Donald Trump, current President of the USA, is a ruthless pursuer of those practices. He financed lower income taxes with deficit, claiming his tax plan favored all. Trump made frequent use of import duties to raise money and support his America First policy He touts the many advantages of tariffs, yet conceals the costs.

An additional approach obfuscating who pays is through free money. This consists of financing promises by printing more money. In old times, creating money was done with a printing press. Nowadays, this is done digitally. Central banks, under control of the government, can, in this fashion, create funds out of thin air. No one's money is taken away by such actions—it so appears to come for free.

In the 1960s, US President Lyndon B. Johnson promised both Butter and Gun. This meant that the social welfare state would be expanded (Butter policy). Simultaneously the USA would step up its intervention in the escalating Vietnam War (Gun policy). He pledged that neither would come at the expense of the other. There would be no trade-off between investments in defense and civilian goods since he financed both by printing money.

Politicians in the German Weimar Republic, shortly after the end of World War I, were also fond of this move. Late in 1922, the Republic failed to pay France an installment of war reparations on time. France responded by occupying the major industrial Ruhr region. German workers launched a general strike on orders of the government. The German executive gave the strikers financial support by printing more and more banknotes. This step gained them a lot of popularity because the majority of Germans resented the French and their occupation of the Ruhr. Furthermore, the money printing didn't seem to cost other Germans outside the Ruhr a single penny.

The charismatic four times Venezuelan President Hugo Chávez won his first election promising a lot of free stuff. He used the Petróleos de Venezuela SA (PDVSA), the state-owned oil and natural gas company, as a piggy bank for his social projects. This caused resentment in the employees of the PDVSA, who felt disadvantaged by Chávez' policy. In 2002, a massive month-long strike broke out at the PVDSA. The lack of fuel crippled the whole transportation system. Hugo Chávez figured out how to manage this situation to great success. He gained in popularity with the Venezuelans through painting the strikers as an entrenched minority that was blocking prosperity for the nation. He then broke the strike and restored order. In the aftermath of the strike, he fired 19,000 striking employees for abandoning their posts. In this way, he took further advantage of the unrest by solidifying his control over the company. By cutting costs and investments in the oil company Chávez secured a sizable war chest. Oil prices thereafter quintupled on the world market. Thanks to those two events, he was next able to finance his generous social programs for a while, long enough to secure re-election in 2006. In that election, he almost doubled the score of his opponent. This is a demonstration of how lucrative it is to exploit a target minority for political gain.

François Mitterrand, in his 1981 campaign for the French presidency, promised in his '110 propositions for France' to introduce a wealth tax. Mitterrand implemented it after his victory, and 1982 saw the creation of the tax on large fortunes. A wealth tax is an example of the **third kind** of strategy. The political appeal is clear: new public spending can be financed at the cost of a small sliver of the population. Such a tax consistently remains a popular measure amid the public. It is less so among economists, but they are only a small part of the electorate anyway. The lesson you should draw is to call during your campaign for such well-liked taxes.

*

These examples can serve as a template and source of inspiration for your own campaign.

*

In summary of this chapter, when composing your message to the people, take popular stances by following polls. Be flexible and adapt to the situation at hand. Your political manifesto should comprise generous promises; you will finance these as previously outlined.

It might be essential to keep some of your pledges if you wish to be re-elected thereafter. But you can worry about that later. The topic of re-election deserves a separate book.

Chapter 3
Claim the country faces grave dangers

I have observed that the man
who despairs when others hope,
is admired by a large class of persons as a sage
— John Stuart Mill

Prepare the content of your campaign by choosing a list of issues you will concentrate on. It is beneficial to pick a list of looming threats for your political manifesto. When campaigning, a savvy candidate exaggerates any perils to the country. He or she insinuates there are grave issues that require immediate and strong action.

There is always something that isn't going well. What if the employment rate has increased, the economy is booming, and crime is down? In that case, you could find a grim alternative danger that requires urgent action. The increasing numbers of single mothers, new technologies, robots, climate change, inequality, or drugs are excellent examples. All past and present polls indicate that a majority of the population is afraid of the future. You need to exploit this feeling if you wish to win.

The world is getting worse

''The country is in a bad state, and will need to be fixed,'' Jair Bolsonaro, President of Brazil, stated in his inauguration speech in 2019. In the National Congress, Bolsonaro described that the most pressing challenge was to rebuild the country. Elizabeth Warren, a favorite at this time of writing in the US Democratic primary for the 2020 election, affirmed ''the middle class has been destroyed and needs to be rebuilt.''

If you listen to any presidential candidate, you get the impression that the world is becoming worse. It seems things are falling apart. This should not surprise you. As Matt Ridley wrote in his book 'The Rational Optimist': ''If you say the world has been getting better you may get away with being called naïve and insensitive. If you say the world is going to go on getting better, you are considered embarrassingly mad. If, on the other hand, you say catastrophe is imminent, you may expect a McArthur genius award or even the Nobel Peace Prize.''

You should hence never run on a platform where you state the country is at a better stage than before (unless you seek re-election). Instead, affirm that the nation is heading towards disaster. After all, if there are no problems, why do voters need your action and leadership? They expect a commander, who faces the latest fashionable crisis in the country and sets forth audacious solutions. So concentrate during your campaign on 1-2 emerging problems and magnify the risks. And denounce your opponents as blind to the danger; or unwilling to tackle them; or insincere in their proposed solutions. The reality is simple: no one ever won a presidential election without melodramatizing.

Note that—regardless if they are left, right, liberal, conservative, and what-not—all winners talked in the same vein about 'regeneration', 'rebuilding', and 'making great again'. And thus you too should include a line about the rebirth or reconstruction of the nation or the world, if you want to succeed. As an integral part of your campaign, claim the country is being destroyed by whatever threat you're trying to protect the people from.

After you have picked this danger, you must be credible and prove you are the best candidate to tackle and resolve the problem. For example, Donald Trump declared he would stand against political correctness. When running for president in 2016, he called it ''the big problem of this country.'' He was credible since he never eschewed controversial statements in the past. He, in this way, garnered and established quite a reputation. Obama was trusted in his position against rising racism, by virtue of his skin color. And Sarkozy was a believable candidate when he ran for the French presidency in 2007 with a platform though on crime. This was because he already gained notoriety with his bold statements as minister of interior. In the past, Sarkozy had stated in front of cameras: ''You've had enough of this bunch of scum [in the ghettos]? Well, we'll get rid of it for you.'' In the eyes of the French voters, there was no doubt Sarkozy would keep his promise. They trusted him on that topic.

Why fear works

Using fear to sell is a tried and true method of the advertising industry. They made this discovery long ago. Ads by hygiene manufacturers make you believe dangerous germs are lurking on every surface. And vehicle manufacturers tout the safety of their cars by showing dramatic car crashes. Fear is a strong feeling which you should employ to manipulate the public to your favor. This potent emotion catches human attention and enhances their memory. Regardless of how intelligent your listeners are, fear will frame their thinking. Keep this effective persuasion technique in your arsenal.

Much can be learned from advertisers when running for president or when ruling your country, by the way. They are a source of inspiration for effective political campaigns. The advertising industry matters because it works. It accounts for close to 1% of GDP in developed countries. The US ad industry employs more than half a million people. Advertisers and marketing departments command over vast resources and enormous budgets. They have spent a considerable amount of time and energy analyzing what works and what doesn't. In their research on consumer manipulation, they discovered many effective tactics. These have become staples of the advertising industry.

Many scientists have as well studied the topic of fear. All their experiments have demonstrated that fear or expected danger activates the limbic system. The limbic system is, from an evolutionary perspective, one of the oldest parts of the brain. It doesn't support higher-level cognitive functions such as mathematics, logic, or speech. Instead, it handles and regulates our primal emotions. It is the animal part of the brain. Gloomy predictions grab the attention of the limbic system. This affects all humans, and is caused by our evolutionary history. Back when we were living in small tribes of hunter-gatherers, any information of impending danger was valuable for survival.

It comes as no surprise then that sect leaders prophesying the end of the world or investment gurus predicting a stock market crash fascinate so many people. It is also the reason why the press reports much more often about negative than positive events. Since fear and doom captivate the audience.

Newspapers are filled with stories of murder, and disasters always make headlines. The staffs of newspapers are no more dark or pessimistic than us. But without this, they wouldn't sell as much and go bankrupt. Climate crisis, a murder case, nuclear proliferation, overpopulation, Ebola, terrorism, etcetera, hence frequently feature on the cover page.

Aspiring the presidency, you should not be a boring person that says everything will be fine. That is not going to land you the job. Instead, use human instincts to your advantage, just like the press and the advertising industry do. Elections are won through pathos, as detailed in Chapter I. A smart candidate thus seeks to hijack the limbic part of the brain.

Let's look at some historical examples of victorious presidential campaigns. Winning candidates were during their electoral campaign successful in arousing public fear. Each possessed elements in their message to exploit the population's concerns.

Case study - The Daisy Ad

An excellent study case is an advertisement for the Democratic candidate Lyndon B. Johnson in the 1964 US presidential campaign. Johnson was running against the Republican Barry Goldwater, who campaigned on a right-wing platform. Goldwater wished to pursue aggressive military action against the communistic Soviet Union.

The Daisy ad

In the advertisement of Johnson, a little girl counts the petals of a daisy flower "1...2...9". When reaching 9, a nuclear missile launch countdown starts. The girl freezes and looks in the distance. A bright flash and a thunderous nuclear mushroom cloud is shown. "Vote Johnson [...] The stakes are too high," a voice says.

The ad follows a classical approach that you should adopt as well:

(1) There is a grave danger—in this case, nuclear Armageddon;

(2) My opponent is in denial of the risks and incapable of handling the threat;

(3) I alone can solve it.

The Daisy ad is considered to have been a determining factor in Johnson's landslide victory in 1964. It was so successful that subsequent candidates outright reused it (Mondale 1984, Dole 1996, Clinton 2016).

The danger is near

''We are running out of oil,'' exclaimed Jimmy Carter in 1976 during the presidential debate. Shrinking oil reserves and expanding consumption will inevitably lead to a massive shortage. As part of his core message to the voters, he claimed only he showed concern; only he would tackle the problem. And Carter accused his opponent, Gerald Ford, of being a dangerously ignorant and wishful thinker. After Carter won the election, he pressed ahead with the theme.

In April 1977, Carter doubled down in a national broadcast to the Americans: ''Unless profound changes are made to lower oil consumption, we now believe that early in the 1980s the World will be demanding more oil than it can produce. [...] We have no choice about that. [...] If we fail to act soon, we will face an economic, social, and political crisis that will threaten our free institutions.''

A menace should not be too far away. Carter didn't affirm that the USA would run out of oil in 100 years, but that the threat was 5 to 10 years ahead. Voters tend to discard or discount perils that are too far in the future. A candidate with strong political acumen would hence exaggerate the urgency. You can then use this vague concept of a faraway danger to push for very concrete and immediate policy proposals. Voters will appreciate that you emphatically voiced your concerns. And they will fume at your opponent's apparent blindness to the dangers.

Exploiting terrorism

An additional theme is—as always—terrorism. In the aftermath of an attack, your rivals will make statements on the situation to profile themselves. You should avoid being pushed on the defensive. Instead, immediately use such events to the benefit of your political campaign. The ubiquitous coverage of the media propagates the horror and panic of the terrorist attack across the whole country.

In recent times, this trend has been accentuated by social media, where onlookers post videos of the attack itself. Some terrorists have even used social media to live-stream their deeds. Everyone will know about the event and expects you to make a statement. Thus remain prepared on this topic, should another (un)expected drama occur. And if your adversary downplays a danger such as terrorism, hit back with all your strength. You should promptly claim that your opponent is hallucinatory and obscene. The latest decades have been marked by 9/11 in the US, and ISIS and Al Qaida in Europe, Africa, and the Middle East.

In his bid for the 2008 US Republican Party nomination, Tom Tancredo released a campaign ad against terrorism. The ad contained graphic images of terrorist attacks in Spain and England. "Vote against spineless politicians. Vote Tancredo... before it's too late." And when Obama wanted to close

Guantanamo Bay, the Republican Party launched a ferocious offensive against him. They claimed that ''Obama wants to bring terrorists on US soil.'' This was technically true, as Obama had to transfer the prisoners of Guantanamo bay to some other prison, in case the former would have been closed. But the clever framing of the Republican Party did not mention these terrorists were already taken prisoner.

''The terrorism in our cities threaten our very way of life,'' Donald Trump said at the RNC. ''Any politician who does not grasp this danger is not fit to lead our country. Americans watching this address tonight have seen the recent images of violence in our streets and the chaos in our communities. Many have witnessed this violence personally; some have even been its victims.'' It is interesting that Trump implicitly acknowledges that many were scared through traditional and social media (''many witnessed personally'') but only a few casualties (''some victims''). Trump continued, ''I have a message for all of you: the crime and violence that today afflicts our nation will soon come to an end. Beginning on January 20th 2017, safety will be restored.'' Notice the implicit three-step approach, already mentioned in our case study:

(1) There is a grave menace—namely terrorism in the cities;

(2) My opponents are in denial of the risks and incapable of handling the threat;

(3) I alone can fix it.

Erdogan, when running for president in Turkey, always hammered on the topic of terrorism, but adjusted to his present enemies. In his victory speech, he affirmed that ''Turkey had chosen to fight decisively against terrorist groups, such as PKK and FETO.'' These two groups coincided with two political opponents of Erdogan: The PKK are Kurdish separatists from eastern Turkey. And FETO is an alleged terrorist group of Erdogan's former ally Gülen. And so the topic of terrorism can be harnessed to your advantage. See it as a political opportunity where you can employ hysteria to the benefit of your cause.

Decline and nostalgia

The strategy described in this chapter even works outside the realm of politics. Oswald Spencer, a German author and historian, published in 1918 his magnum opus 'Der Untergang des Abendlandes' ('The Decline of the West', or more correctly translated as 'The Downfall of the West'). The book was a wild success and catapulted Spengler to fame. By his contemporaries, he was deemed the most significant intellectual of the first half of the 20th century. In Germany, the work's thesis was widely discussed, and translations soon spread across the globe. Spengler's ideas exerted immense influence in the 1920s. Among well-educated, the whole discourse became oriented around Spengler's thesis: Western Civilization was in decline.

In his model of history, each culture has a limited and predictable lifespan. Western Civilization, according to his model, would inevitably decay and rot. He forecast the downfall by the year 2000. This decline resembles our own physical and mental deterioration with age. Only a 'Caesar' could save our civilization, he claimed. Oswald Spencer could have been a successful politician. None of his predictions have come true, nor have any of his historical models shown any value. But he played into the prevailing pessimism and the fear of impending decline. His book contained few logos but is full of pathos and a bit of ethos (a pure, strong, and noble Caesar can still save us).

Despite that by all metrics, life today is better than 50, 20 or even 10 years ago, a majority long to an idealized past. These false memories of happy days gone by, also called nostalgia, can be manipulated to the benefit of your campaign. Why is this emotion so potent?

Firstly, the impending doom and decline is one reason people experience nostalgia. The future is bleak, full of dangers and obstacles, as you should be reminding your voters of. The fear and uncertainty about the future are always present. (The Germans express this type of anxiety with a single word, 'Zukunftangst'.) People in the past seem to have lived a happy, carefree life. Somehow, voters forget that 50 years ago, people also faced challenges and a multitude of dangers. Observe that many of those past challenges were overcome, and many threats never materialized. It is the reason why it from today's perspective, the previous generation had it easier. People compare the unknown, undetermined future with the known, determined past.

The second reason why nostalgia works and you should appeal to it is because humans have a faulty memory. People long for an idealized bygone era because they don't remember well how it was. Scientific studies have demonstrated that our recollection of the past is unreliable at best and malleable at worst. A mere song can evoke strong emotions of nostalgia and completely bias our remembrance of events. Our thoughts are selective and self-serving, yet all of us have high confidence in our recollections. Our memories feel so accurate; we rarely doubt even the details. Social scientists and psychologists, however, have studied our memories and found them often inaccurate or downright false. Improvements in DNA analysis have also allowed us to revisit many past crime cases. For instance, several convictions where sure-fire eyewitness accounts were often decisive, were reversed based on this new DNA technology. Scientists euphemistically say that human memory is adaptive and flexible. I advise readers to hold a diary precisely for this reason. Write daily down your ideas, feelings, and thoughts. After a couple of years, when rereading your journal, you will be amazed at what you wrote. You will realize that your present-self will interpret past events differently than your past-self.

Thirdly, many people feel a loss of status or a drop in their standard of living; this can be real or imagined. They think the modern world has empowered others, some outside groups, or some individuals, though not them. They recall the old times as a time where they were more respected. Times when privacy wasn't trampled by big tech, when inequality was lower, when people still had faith in God, when more people were unionized, when there was no civil rights act, when companies didn't dodge taxes, when there still was the draft, when the Chinese didn't pollute the Earth, when there were no hippies, or when there still were hippies, when there were fewer immigrants, when people bought locally, when there was no global warming, when the state of Israel didn't exist yet, when divorces were almost non-existent, and abortion too, etcetera. For all colors, flavors, and political sentiments, something was allegedly better back in past times.

If you wish to win, capitalize on nostalgia for the benefit of your presidential bid. As an illustration of its mad power: large swaths of the electorate in Eastern Europe recall fondly communist times. Communist parties often score more than 20% in modern-day elections. But in reality, the communist, totalitarian regime that ruled over Eastern Europe, excelled at nothing except repression, generating poverty, and the construction of walls. Eastern Europe lived in those days under constant fear of invasion by its own ally, the Soviet Union. This was for once not an unrealistic fear, as several of such invasions took place: East-Germany (1953), Hungary (1956), Czech Republic (1968).

The best example of an excellent application of this nostalgia tactic is, without any doubt, the political campaign of Vote Leave. This was the organization that pushed the United Kingdom to leave the European Union. With their ''Take Back Control'' slogan, which summarized the core message of Vote Leave, they spoke to a sense of loss. British citizens recall the times when Britain was an empire that ruled over a quarter of the globe, a message they have been spoon-fed at school. They regret this loss of status. But they also deplore the loss of an imagined and romanticized sense of social harmony and homeliness that once existed in Britain. The well-led Vote Leave campaign encouraged dreams of restoring this past and so won the Brexit Referendum.

Truth is not your objective, but power is. Politics has never been a matter of reason. Persuasion techniques based on sentiments, as detailed in the Introduction, are the most powerful. You have to employ them if you wish to win. Exploiting nostalgia is an effective tool to arouse emotions; keep in your toolkit and apply it when designing your political manifesto and slogan.

Saving the environment

You could adopt the protection of the environment as a cornerstone of your program. The human destruction of nature is not a recent development. While the modern pro-environment movement started to gain traction in the 1980s, there are many predecessors to it. Environmentalism (which is often called ecology in Europe) is the ideological movement that asserts humankind should carry out more actions to protect nature. That otherwise, the fragile symbiosis between Humans and Earth will shatter. Humankind is on the edge of environmental catastrophe, the movement declares.

This idea has existed in different parts of the world throughout history. More than two thousands year ago, old Jainist religious text in India promoted symbiosis between all living beings and the preservation of nature. In 18th century India, hundreds of Bishnois Hindus went to their deaths trying to protect trees from being cut by their lord. This inspired in the 1970s the Chipko movement, a pro-tree group that originated in India and has exerted worldwide influence. By the end of the 19th-century, pro-conservation clubs sprang up all across the US and Europe. Particularly popular was bird-conservation. After the extinction of the passenger pigeon (*Ectopistes migratorius*), the theme reached the highest political levels. In 1916, the US and Canada signed the Protection of Migratory birds Convention. Natural Parks Service sprang up in 1916 in the USA, and the Forestry Commission was established in 1919 in Britain. Germany followed suit in the 1930s with the Reichsnaturschutzgesetz and passed a stringent animal protection law. Already in the past, the fear of destruction of nature has played a role in politics.

Although he was not a politician, Malthus was the first modern person to preach environmental catastrophe to great effect. He became one of the most famous English scholars, after writing 'An Essay on the Principle of Population' in 1798. In his book, Malthus predicted that the exponential growth of human population would soon clash with the limited resources on Earth. He concluded that humanity would face disaster and mass warfare for the few remaining means. Malthus proposed to keep the total human population within resource limits. This would be achieved on the one hand through naturally occurring famine, disease, and disasters. And on the other hand, through active birth control, postponement of marriage, and celibacy. The theme of overpopulation was also central in the 'The Limits to Growth' report from 1972, which sold 30 million copies. It echoed Malthus and foresaw impending doom.

As said at the beginning of this chapter, you should exaggerate the menaces to your country. Your campaign should pound on this grave issue. And state it requires (your) immediate and forceful action. Exploit the anxiety of citizens on a theme and then present yourself as their savior.

The modern 21st century variation of environmental collapse is climate change (also known as global warming). Already some persons have profited from this latest threat to become presidents such as Evo Morales in Bolivia and Alexander Van Der Bellen in Austria. Barack Obama was as well a frequent user of this talking point, albeit it wasn't a decisive issue in American politics yet. This theme is in the 21st century, without a doubt, a good foundation for your campaign. You, too, could choose this topic as a key element in your presidential campaign, once the polls indicate it is on the public's mind.

How to turn this subject into an effective addition to your message? It is hard to follow the news without increasing mention of natural disasters such as droughts, floods, or tropical cyclones. Every year, it seems, the weather breaks new records. The frequency of such news has risen, such that a crisis appears near. The IPCC (Intergovernmental Panel on Climate Change) in 2018 wrote: ''There is low confidence in attribution of changes in tropical cyclone activity to human influence''. And it further wrote that: ''There is low confidence in attributing changes in drought over global land areas since the mid-20th century to human influence.''

In spite of this information, you should highlight any extreme weather event as proof of the climate emergency. Droughts, hurricanes—claim all occur because of climate change. The reason is that the electorate is more impressed by floods, droughts, tropical cyclones, and heat waves than by the average worldwide temperature. The sea-level rise is also a suitable angle; you can evoke the nightmarish image of waves swallowing land. Presidential campaigns are won with pathos, not with logos. Headlines of disasters grab the attention; an average projected temperature difference by the end of the century does not. People do not have time to check out all claims on global averages or acquire a Ph.D. in the subject. In contrast, extreme events are salient. They are very visible and will, therefore, generate more fear and attention.

The danger of climate change has been gaining awareness, which is why we will see more candidates adopt it. Alexander van der Bellen was elected President of Austria in 2016. He affirmed that ''This generation is the last that can tackle the global climate crisis.'' US President Barack Obama in his State of the Union in 2015, in the same vein: ''Climate change is the greatest threat to future generations.'' And more: ''There's one issue that will define the contours of this century more dramatically than any other, and that is the urgent and growing threat of a changing climate.''

Obama's wording can serve as a blueprint for your speeches. Adopt this template (''urgent and growing threat'', ''dramatic issue of this century'') for any theme, not only climate change. It follows the standard approach described in this chapter. Obama also warned of ''Mass Migrations'' if we don't confront climate change. Migration is another great topic that I will discuss in more detail in the next chapter.

Foreign influence

Another element you could include in your message to the nation is insinuating that your opponent is in the hands of foreign powers. For example, during the French presidential campaign, Emmanuel Macron claimed Russian hackers targeted his movement. And he asserted that his opponent, Marine Le Pen, was a puppet of the Kremlin, for she received a loan for her campaign from a state-owned Russian bank.

During the Cold War, neutral third world nations would see regular interference and influence of their electoral processes by the United States or the Soviet Union. Notwithstanding the fall of the Soviet-Union, claiming your opponent is a puppet in the hand of foreign powers remains a powerful tool you should keep in your arsenal.

This class of argument performs wonders in less developed countries. The 2018 presidential election in Mexico saw the victory of the National Regeneration Movement (MORENA) from López Obrador. López Obrador declared that Mexico had become a worse place over time. This happened, he said, due to the rampant corruption encouraged by his predecessor and political opponents. A national regeneration was now required. Before the election, López Obrador accused the International Monetary Fund of being an accomplice to corruption in Mexican politics. He claimed that the IMF's policies are responsible for poverty, unemployment, and violence in the country. López Obrador promised that if he won the presidency, Mexico would follow "its own agenda," instead of that of alleged foreign interests. His opponents, at their turn, tried in vain to convince voters that a López Obrador victory would turn Mexico into another Venezuela. They also accused him of being backed by Venezuela, Cuba, and Russia. And Nicolas Maduro in the Venezuelan 2018 election blamed all the country's woes on the United States of America and declared that all his opponents were dancing to the tune of Washington. Evo Morales, multiple times President of Bolivia, expressed similar beliefs: "Some countries of Europe have to free themselves from the US Empire. They [The US Empire] are not going to frighten us because we are a people with dignity and sovereignty."

In all these cases, presidents managed to capitalize on the fear of foreign and powerful nations. These are typically the USA or international institutions such as the IMF.

You might be running on a pro-European platform, as most notably did Emmanuel Macron in 2017. If so, you shall credit the

European Union as the main reason there has not been a war in Europe. Other factors were more decisive: nuclear weapons or the USA's leadership of NATO. Nevertheless, don't mention those because European voters like neither of them. Declare that anti-EU contenders are a grave danger for peace. The specter of the world wars you will evoke so scares away swing voters from voting for your opponent.

Of course, this only applies if you have taken a pro-EU stance. If you take the other path, you can also spook the public. It is attractive to denounce the EU bureaucracy and alleged corruption in Brussels because people don't like bureaucrats in another country deciding their fate. The lobbying, the absurdly high salaries of the EU civil servants, the lack of transparency, are all promising angles of attack. Declare Brussels is secretly amassing more power. And you must suggest the image of Brussels slowly chocking the member states. Or evoke the image of a frog gradually being cooked in warm water (because of the gradual transition of the temperature, the frog doesn't realize it until too late). Whereas you are their savior; you will defend the common man against the bureaucratic elite.

Dangers of technology

A final popular theme to impress the electorate is the danger of new science or technology. Nuclear power plants, fracking, or GMOs are good cases. GMOs (genetically modified organisms), for example, is an excellent avenue of attack against your opponents. Despite scientific consensus that GMOs pose no more risk than other food, the public remains distrustful of the new technology. The European Union disregarded the report of its own scientist council, which concluded that GMOs pose no inherent risks. They next introduced bans, moratoriums, and stringent regulation. Yet when your opponents would happen to support such types of technology, denounce them. Evoke the powerful emotion of disgust by highlighting the presumed health dangers to humans and nature. Just like many people hate eating something weird such as insects, so can the idea of genetically modified food arouse revulsion. By appealing to disgust, you will awake an intuitive, deep-seated negative response. People ultimately trust their 'gut feeling'; exploit it for your own political gain.

Bolivian President Evo Morales applied the insight that people distrust technology, especially in the area of nutrition. In a speech at the inauguration of conference on climate change, he said: ''Baldness appears to be normal is a disease in Europe, almost all of them are bald, and that is because of the things they eat; while among the indigenous peoples there are no bald people, because we eat other things.'' And also that other countries were destroying Earth, he called this ''ecocide.'' Moreover, he stated that ''Capitalism is like a cancer for Mother Earth.'' In this way, scared voters gathered behind him and carried him four times to the presidency.

Talk about what is on people's minds

It is crucial in your campaign to choose the threat to your country wisely. Pick something the population is familiar with. Select the menace based on current events and polls of what worries the people. You have to namely pick the peril that is on most people's minds.

Ecologist parties failed in their first decades (1970s-1980s) because people were unfamiliar with climate change. In the meantime, the topic is widely discussed in schools and the media, which makes it an excellent pick. Already some candidates won with it and likely several will follow.

An excellent illustration of a wise pick is Lyndon B. Johnson implying his opponent would cause nuclear Armageddon—as seen in the case study above. This was in 1964, at the height of the Cold War. The Cuban Missile Crisis had taken place a year before. Less than 20 years earlier, nuclear weapons destroyed Hiroshima and Nagasaki. It was therefore a topic fresh on everyone's mind.

*

The strategy addressed in this chapter should not be your only one. A promising candidate often needs to have more than one string to their bow. It is, of course, useful to spark enthusiasm in the crowd, as it will motivate your followers to talk about you to their friends and family. A loyal base with active participation is always an asset. But simultaneous to enthusiasm, also exploit fear. Fear stimulates vigilance and skepticism towards your opponents. At the same time, it will facilitate persuasion from your side. Hence your message should contain at least one looming threat to the nation.

Chapter 4
Blame a minority

See now, how men lay blame upon us gods
for what is after all nothing but their own folly
— Homer, Odyssey (tr. Samuel Butler)

As part of the blueprint of a successful campaign, you should always find a minority to blame. On every issue, be it crime, jobs, or the place of your country in the world, bash that single outnumbered group. By concentrating the blame, you will cause the least amount of dissatisfaction among the entire population. You also give a simple explanation for the country woes and provide an actionable plan to deal with it.

It is a mistake to share the blame over many groups (farmers, hippies, immigrants, bankers, LGBTQ, ...), as this will cause many to hold a grudge and resent you. In contrast, by accusing a single minority over and over again, only they will oppose you. You can then use their ferocious hostility and animosity as proof of their guilt.

This minority should not be too significant. If it is too large, their vote might swing the election result. Yet the group should not be too small or insignificant because its members need to be a credible threat. You should aim for 1-3% of the population range. The CEOs, a particular immigrant, religious, or ethnic group, the bankers; all are excellent targets.

With the help of polls, as seen in a previous chapter, shape your strategy. If jobs are the top priority of the electorate, reproach immigrants from stealing jobs and depressing wages. If failing banks are on top of everyone's minds, bash bankers. If people are concerned about rising healthcare prices, pledge to dismantle the wicked pharmaceutical cartel; vow to tackle their price gouging. Detect any anxiety that lies under the surface of the voters and amplify it. Give the masses what they want, by promising to crush that minority group that stands in the way.

I am not advocating those policies, but merely drawing attention to what works and what not. This is not a text about ethics but rather a cookbook that explains the steps required to (legally) grasp control. I abstain from morals or good policy in this text and prefer to leave those to wiser authors. As written before, the focus lies on what is required to win.

Immigrant group

An immigrant group is often ideal because they are outnumbered, and fewer of them have voting rights. This means you won't lose many votes by criticizing them, since that group only accounts for a small percentage of the electorate. It is wise to pick only one subgroup of immigrants. That way, you can defend yourself against racist charges by pointing out how much you love the other immigrant groups.

When running in the USA, a nation that always had a lot of immigration, one can pick from many groups. In the 19th century, for example, the Irish were a popular target of presidential candidates. The Irish were poor, stole jobs, and were violent and criminal. Furthermore, they were Catholics, therefore loyal to the pope instead of being faithful to the Republic. This gave many angles of attack: crime, jobs, social welfare, or subversion of US foreign policy.

Franklin Delano Roosevelt, half a century later, restricted immigration from Germany (cutting down the number of accepted refugees by 90% in 1940), and interned Japanese immigrants. He also proceeded to make a deal with Mexico, the Bracero Program, which allowed many Mexicans to be employed in the USA.

In the 21st century, Donald Trump turned the tables around: "When Mexico sends its people, they're not sending the best. They're sending people that have lots of problems [...]. They're bringing drugs. They're bringing crime. They're rapists. And some, I assume, are good people." This is an excellent illustration of how to charge a group of immigrants. There is indeed a lot of crime and an opioid use epidemic in the USA that people wish to see resolved. By blaming Mexicans, Trump provides a simple explanation for the country woes and an actionable plan to deal with it. In case he is accused of overgeneralizing, the last sentence keeps a certain amount of plausible deniability.

Let's look at other immigration cases across the world.

"The scum of the earth is showing up in Brazil, as if we didn't have enough problems of our own to sort out," said Jair Bolsonaro before becoming President of Brazil. He became more nuanced during the actual election. Then he pledged to leave the UN migration pact, yet also to support Venezuelan refugees. Four million Venezuelans fled the country's communist regime, and a large chunk sought refuge in Brazil. This balanced approach, of blaming some but not all immigrants, has worked well for many candidates.

In South Korea, a mere 500 Yemenis fleeing the civil war asked for asylum in 2018. President Moon Jae-in, who is a former human right lawyer, was at first in favor of accepting a small number of refugees. But a petition demanding the government not accept the refugees garnered more than 700,000 signatures. Moon Jae-in was already under pressure for his failed economic reforms and the rising unemployment among youth. He pivoted on the issue, swiftly tightening up visa requirements for Yemenis and bashing the 'fake refugees'. The opinion polls have since then swung back up. Remember, presidential campaigns are about pathos. Don't try to counter the passions of people, but surf on them instead.

In Europe, past presidential candidates have tried to blame all middle-eastern newcomers. They bashed them on their animal cruelty, crime, unemployment, allegiance to ISIS, and many other topics. Till now, this has been without much success. The reason why it hasn't worked is twofold. First, this minority has acquired voting rights, and now their vote plays too large of a role. Second, the candidates appear racist, which scares away voters. When shaping your political program, it is better to proceed with a more targeted offensive on a smaller subgroup. Fewer would then oppose you, and you can keep plausible denial in the face of accusations of racism.

The Danish social-democrats are a successful exception in Europe. They have over the last years carried out persuasive anti-immigrant rhetoric while escaping allegations of racism. The Danish social democrats have navigated those waters with great care so that accusations of ethnic or religious discrimination wouldn't tarnish their image. During their campaign, they announced their intention to cut benefits for immigrants. This discourse culminated in a victory in the 2019 elections, where they became the largest party and secured the post of prime minister. That is impressive in an era where most other social-democratic parties in Europe are suffering reverses.

The key to their success was that they pledged to defend and extend the social welfare state. This policy enjoyed broad support in Denmark. Simultaneously, they supported applying different rules for non-citizens. They voted in favor of a bill allowing Danish authorities to confiscate jewelry, money, and other valuable items from refugees crossing the border. And they further excluded them for a period from unemployment benefits, child support, and educational assistance. This message was very effective in gaining the public's vote. The voters liked it because this saves the welfare state for the Danish (the majority) at the expense of immigrants (who are part of a minority and don't have voting rights to boot).

The rich and corporations

An excellent potential target are the wealthy. The wealthy have many uses since you can charge them for everything: global warming, (white-collar) crime, poverty, inequality, job losses, and so forth. When drafting your manifesto, it is, however, a mistake to simply blame 'the rich'. This term is namely too vague and much broader than it seems. Accusations against the 1% most affluent citizens might alienate a substantial part of the electorate. This is because, although the majority of people are not part of the 1%, many believe (rightfully or not) they will join the 1% at one point. Furthermore, large parts of the electorate have friends or family in the 1%.

Let's note that young adults have lower incomes and occasionally debt, but will grow richer with time. This happens as a natural consequence of rising incomes with experience, paying off debt, saving for the future, or inheritance. Many individuals will hence at one point reach the top 1%, even if at a given point in time, few are within the top. As a result, phrases like ''It is time to make the government work for all of us… and not the 1%'' are not winning phrases. Another issue is that the middle-class fears that a part of taxes will fall on their shoulders. They know the rich are clever in circumventing tax burdens. Most past taxes on the rich eventually landed on the middle-class too. So, when you produce policy proposals, confirm that the proposed taxes could not possibly affect the middle-class.

That is why it is better to target those ''truly, truly rich''. You have to clarify to the people that you aim at the top 0.01% or so. That way, you will neither alienate those who think they will get rich one day, nor those in the middle class. Elizabeth Warren has heeded this advice and structured her message along those lines. ''The ultra-rich have rigged our economy and rigged our tax rules. We need structural change. That's why I'm proposing something brand-new: An annual wealth tax on the tippy-top 0.1%.'' Notice how she doesn't target the rich but only the ultra-rich.

Pretend the affluent act in unison. They are plotting their continued enrichment on the back of hardworking, ordinary people. They conspire at Davos and the yearly Bilderberg Meeting, coordinating their plans. If you have chosen to run on a left-wing platform, you could claim they are secretly lobbying for more free trade and depressing employee wages. From a right-wing angle, you can accuse them of encouraging immigration and undermining the nation-state. If you have chosen the centrist path, you can wield both sides' arguments.

You could also criticize neoliberalism or condemn corporations. These are already more abstract concepts, and hence fewer people will have scruples hating them. Some individuals namely still have qualms despising other humans and don't want to appear jealous, one of the cardinal sins. Nevertheless, they have no remorse bashing companies, especially big companies, and for sure if those happen to be big, foreign companies. Targeting rich, international companies is an excellent tactic. It combines blaming the rich, blaming corporations, and blaming foreigners. Each of the single elements is a good element for an attack. And the combination has been a source of popularity for many politicians.

In recent times, the French President Emmanuel Macron scored points with his anti-internet-giant tax. While the tax, in theory, applies to all giant internet companies, it is common knowledge that it falls in practice on a few successful American corporations. And same with Margrethe Vestager, a Danish politician serving as the European Commissioner for Competition since 2014: she always struck at American companies and thereby gained a lot in popularity with the European electorate. Yet when it came to investigating Volkswagen's fraud, a European car company that breached environmental norms, all those European politicians governing the institutions were conspicuously absent.

Another abstract concept in the same vein is automation. Anticipating the future, I envision robots will steal human jobs. A study from the Brookings Institution, in 2019, reported that one-quarter of all American jobs are at a high risk of automation and replacement by artificial intelligence (AI) by 2030. Since robots don't vote and people don't have qualms hating machinery, they are an ideal target. The 19th-century Luddite movement was already based on hostility towards the industrial revolution; they would storm factories to destroy textile machinery therein.

Foreigners

Condemning foreigners is a bit different from criticizing immigration. While immigrants are already in your country, and some might even have acquired voting rights over time, foreigners are abroad. Accusing foreigners is often a smart mode of operation, since they don't vote and their voice is less heard in both traditional and social media. Promising politicians usually apply this tactic. For instance, the Germans were scolded during the financial crisis in Southern Europe, the Chinese blamed in recent times in the USA, and the Jews condemned by newly elected officials in the Middle East.

The last one became pretty much a mandatory step in one's political career in that region. So, dear reader, if you are aspiring public office in the Middle East, follow the example of former President of Iran Ahmadinejad whose aversion for Israel was no secret. He would often denounce and make flashy statements about Israel. Stirring the emotions of the electorate against your nation's presumed archenemy is a reliable tactic to gain voters. It can also serve as a diversion when you are criticized on another topic. If a pesky journalist asks you a question you don't like, in case of doubt, blame Israel, no matter what. Voting is a statement. This means voters experience a feel-good feeling when they punish those they don't like—it is about pathos. The electorate will admire you for lashing out against Israel and reward you in the polling booth.

Remember to claim that the target minority is conspiring and exerts considerable influence behind the scenes. You will protect the right people and punish the bad guys. You are not one of their puppets, contrary to other presidential candidates. Parts of the population believe in conspiracies. They do so because they think it makes them smart. By disbelieving traditional media (which anyways are biased if not outright controlled) and discarding common knowledge, they show a skeptical and critical mind. A skeptical and critical mindset is a telltale signal of a scientific and intelligent person, so they believe.

Why blaming works

Prejudice and stereotypes are, to some extent, the natural application of Bayesian statistics. This mathematical method tells you that, for example, should most criminals come from a specific neighborhood, it is probable that the perpetrator who commits the next crime is also from that neighborhood. Though this method gives no proof or certitude. It only indicates probabilities and requires robust data to function well. Yet psychological research has shown that humans are too often swayed by loyalty to their own kind. Therefore, they don't apply statistical methods correctly to outside groups. This is a form of distortion of kinship support that existed when we were living as small groups of hunter-gatherers. It still lives on in our genes, despite the drastic change of society. This loyalty leads all humans to apply biased filters on the events of life.

Blame also serves as a self-defense mechanism. For example, a fervent and prejudiced supporter of the Democratic Party might think an anecdotal mistake of a Republican is caused by his or her evilness. An error from a fellow Democrat, in contrast, is merely an unfortunate mishap, from which no generalization can be made. And so one's psychological self-worth is protected, whereas the criticism of other groups is justified. This motivated reasoning allows us to keep our believes.

Another mechanism that explains the effectiveness of blaming is that people sometimes panic and then search for simple solutions. In the 16-17th century, sporadic witch scares broke out in Europe and the Americas. Lone and weird women were accused of witchcraft and, after that, burned at the stake. These were satisfactory victims for an ecstatic crowd looking to let off some steam.

Hence—to attain the highest office—call to the jealousy of the electorate, their fear, their greed, their hate, and criticize a handful or a small group. Declare that the minority blocks the prosperity of the people. And don't be fooled: nobody ever won without applying those ruses. Past presidents and candidates have handled those psychological devices too, as a look at their campaigns and speeches demonstrates. All selected at least one minority to blame the country's woes upon.

Portia's gambit

'Portia's gambit' is a useful stratagem to exploit these psychological findings. It is one of the oldest tricks in the world, yet it keeps working over and over again. This stratagem is named after a personage from Shakespeare's 'The Merchant of Venice'. This strategy is terrific when your country is heavily indebted to foreigners. Accuse your debtors of being dumb and greedy; they don't understand the (Christian) values of mercy and forgiveness.

You will call them foreign "vultures" and "hyenas" and ask for the annulment of the debt. Once you have grasped power, you will default on all loans to them.

Portia's gambit has been applied so often in past and recent history that many examples abound. Argentina has defaulted to the dismay of its lenders already several times, and it has somehow grown to a habit. The country limps from default and crisis to the next one, with almost farcical repetition. Especially presidents and candidates of the dominant Peronist movement (an Argentinian ideological movement, named after President Juan Perón) are quite apt at blaming foreign creditors and the IMF for Argentina's financial crises.

Less extreme was the example of Syriza led by Alexis Tsipras. He promised to reject austerity, restructure the national debt, and otherwise threatened to default to the Troika. The Greek population loved this message. In this way, he captured 49% of the Greek Parliament and most of the executive branch in 2015. He ultimately, though, did not carry those menaces out once he held power.

Another case is from Iceland. During the Great Financial Crisis in 2008, Iceland's banking system collapsed. More than 300,000 British and Dutch who held savings with the Icelandic Landsbanki saw their accounts frozen. This lead to the Icesave Case, a diplomatic dispute with the UK and the Netherlands. Both states requested a repayment from Iceland. The Icelandic Parliament, called the Althing, agreed twice to do so, but the President exerted twice his veto. Ólafur Grímsson, President of Iceland, knew that people resented paying loans back to foreigners. Two referendums backed him against the Althing, to the dismay of the British and the Dutch. Intelligent application of

Portia's gambit so secured Ólafur Grímsson's re-election. He ended up with a record five terms and twenty years in office.

The media and political elites

It might also happen that the press doesn't favor you, or you pretend it is so. That hasn't stopped candidates from winning, so it is an approach you could consider following. Insist the media is biased and in the pocket of your adversary. ''It is not true that Pena is 20 points above me. It's part of the management of the regime. They have control of the media, with few exceptions,'' said Andres Manuel López Obrador in the Mexican presidential campaign.

It is essential not to appear to be losing, which might demotivate your supporters and the undecided from voting for you. Furthermore, those that are winning in the polls draw more media attention. And a majority of the population adheres to a 'winning-proves-the-candidate-is-right' mentality. This creates a bandwagon effect, where candidates that are gaining in the polls, in a self-fulfilling prophecy, keep surging. That is why appearing to be winning is so important.

Cristina de Kirchner, who was elected president with the largest margin of victory in Argentinian history, also had a turbulent relationship with the press. She maintained that journalistic objectivity does not exist and that all journalists act on behalf of certain interests. The rise of social media has made eschewing the traditional media a much more potent approach.

The common people seldom like or trust the political elite. A Gallup poll in August 2019 found that only 17% of the Americans approved the work done by politicians in the US Congress; 79% disapproved, and 5% held no opinion.

It is a strong play on ethos (arguments based on an individual's credibility) to denounce the political elite. This class ticks the boxes: they are not too numerous but arguably influential. If you are an outsider, which will strengthen your claim, consider running against the political establishment. You should then fuel dissatisfaction with the system and sow distrust of mainstream political elites. Donald Trump is yet again a master of this tactic. During his campaign, he insisted that Washington was ''broken.'' Only an outsider could tame Washington and fix it so that the power is put back where it belongs—with the people.

Cultural subgroups

Blaming cultural subgroups is also a winner. The Nixon campaign in 1968 won the US election in part by putting the blame on the hippies for the woes of the country. Hippies didn't support the troops in Vietnam, dodged the draft, and caused rising drug consumption, Nixon asserted. For his re-election, Nixon doubled down and declared ''War on Drugs'' (which still last till today), to target the hippies. Wielding a correct blaming strategy, he was re-elected by a landslide in 1972, taking 60.7% of the popular vote and carrying 49 out of 50 states.

Nixon embraced the right message at the time because hippies were but a small subset of the population, and the Vietnam War provoked high emotions. Pathos was very potent in those circumstances.

Public opinion on soft drugs might, however, shift in the future. Don't forget the advice from a previous chapter; remain prepared to turn your coat when polls indicate that a majority wants decriminalization of soft drugs. Crucial is that you apply the correct tactics described within this chapter, but tailor the content of your political program to the conditions, the time, and the place of your presidential run.

Nicolas Sarkozy gained with a single event enormous name recognition and popularity in 2005 when he was French Minister of Interior. This allowed him later to run for and win the French presidency. On a visit to the city of La Dalle d'Argenteuil on 25 October 2005, he was insulted and victim of stone-throwing by the inhabitants of the district. And in that moment, he declared to the camera: "You've had enough, haven't you, you've had enough of this bunch of scum? Well, we'll get rid of it for you." And as Minister of Interior (and commander of the police), he began blaming the subculture thriving within French ghettos. And he was relentless in his assault, stating boldly "As of tomorrow, we're going to clean up the ghetto with Kärcher [high-pressure washing equipment]. We'll put in the necessary manpower and time, but it will be cleaned up." Riots lasted three weeks and Sarkozy was able to benefit from the events, as it gave him significant press coverage. In the aftermath, a poll from the market research firm Ipsos indicated 68% had favorable opinions of him and his actions.

Divide et Impera

Prudence is required though when drafting your program and preparing your electoral strategy. When you accuse as part of your campaign a minority group that is too large, you run significant risks. Remarkable is the 2015 Sri Lanka election in this regard. Sri Lanka is inhabited in majority by the Sinhalese, who form roughly three-quarters of the population. The most significant minority are the Tamils, who represent more than 10% of the inhabitants. A past civil war between the government and the terrorist Tamil Tigers marks the country's politics. The incumbent Mahinda Rajapaksa was already ruling for ten years in 2015 and seeking re-election. Rajapaksa was expected to win in this still somewhat immature democracy. Blatant violation of electoral law, violence, and media manipulation such as denying opponents air-time tainted the elections.

Maithripala Sirisena was a member of the same party as the incumbent. He defected to the opposition and ran a moderate campaign against his former ally Rajapaksa. In a complete surprise win, Sirisena became President of Sri Lanka with 51% of the vote. Analysis of the results shows that a majority of the Sinhalese voted for Rajapaksa. In contrast, close to nine in ten of the minority voters chose Sirisena. President Rajapaksa had been accused and harassed those minorities over the past years. This became his downfall, although the magnitude was unexpected.

It is vital to pick a small minority target. Preferably this group does not comprise more than 1-3% of the electorate. Targeting a minority exceeding 10-15%, such as the Tamils in Sri Lanka, is a considerable risk, and ill-advised. A more moderate candidate could rise against you and win part of the dominant ethnic group, yet simultaneously secure nearly all of the minority vote, as happened in Sri Lanka.

One more word on Donald Trump. Although he is a political mastermind expert at many tactics described within this book, he must tread carefully with his wide criticism of Hispanics immigrants. Trump will score better in future elections if he only targets a single subgroup of Hispanics. A good example would be the Latinos from Central America (Guatemala, Honduras, Nicaragua, El Salvador). Most of the immigrants crossing the Mexican-American border at this point come from those countries. They are not numerous enough in the electorate to form a significant block. By only targeting them, Trump wouldn't have to face the antagonism of descendants of Mexican immigrants and Puerto Ricans who are much more numerous in the USA. Furthermore, polls have indicated that Mexicans dislike immigrants from Central America as well.

Let yourself instead be inspired by Julius Caesar. He conquered Gaul two thousand years ago by playing the Gallic tribes against themselves. Allied with two Gallic tribes—the Aedui and the Remi—, he proceeded to defeat the other tribes one by one. Trump let an opportunity slip to take a similar approach, which might very well be pivotal for his re-election. He still sometimes tries to appeal to Hispanics by eating Mexican food and posting on Twitter how much he likes it. Despite those acts and statements, many do not experience him as sincere anymore. A more focused approach of targeting Central Americans would be advisable. Trump wouldn't lose so much Hispanic votes to the Democratic Party, while still retaining his base. Mexicans also dislike Guatemalans and such people from Central-America. So by only blaming Guatemalans, Trump would not have raised the suspicion of Americans with Mexican roots.

As a general rule, different immigrant groups dislike each other more than natives do. For example, Kurds and Turks regularly battle in the German and other European cities. And in

Switzerland, there are many immigrant groups from ex-Yugoslavia (Serbs, Albanians/Kosovars, Croats) which remain hostile to each other due to the conflicts of past decades. Violent incidents and provocations are ubiquitous. So instead of making blanket statements condemning all immigrants, target a subset and profit from the internal animosity between these groups. Divide et Impera (divide and rule), as Caesar said.

In summary, it is beneficial to blame a minority in your political campaign. If you aim for the presidency, select the optimal group on which you will put the blame. Pick your target wisely, not too large nor too small. Your political program should then link that minority to other topics such as unemployment, crime, subversion of the nation, and so forth. Poll the people to know what worries them the most. The examples from this chapter can serve as a starting point.

A word of caution though—certain groups have been targeted so often that the public might get tired of blaming them. Innovate and find a new minority to accuse. These can always be found or invented by slicing and dicing the population. Even if the entire country is racially homogeneous, practices the same religion, find something to set them apart, and sort people into buckets. Let your inner creative mind work and explore possibilities. For example, in Flanders (North-Belgium), politicians taking stances against the South-Belgian immigration around Brussels score points. And in Ticino (the Italian speaking part of Switzerland), the popular party 'La Lega' is opposed to Italian immigration, even though no one else can distinguish a Ticinese from an Italian.

Part II -
Get your message across

Chapter 5
Raise money and spend it wisely

Empty pockets never held anyone back.
Only empty heads and empty hearts can do that
— Norman Vincent Peale

Over the past chapters, you have acquired insights on how you should determine the content of your campaign (part I). This is the first steps in all successful runs. It is, at present, essential that you reach voters and communicate your message to them. You have to disseminate information to the electorate about your program and yourself. Raising money for your campaign will enable you to fund a team, buy fliers, ads, and organize events. In this chapter, I will discuss how to manage money, and how to deal with a lack of it.

The role of money

A lot has been written on the topic of campaign finance. First, I have to dispel a myth. Reform advocates complain with exaggerated rhetoric about the influence of money in politics. But, contrary to popular belief, the funds raised by a candidate don't materially affect the outcome of the election. Candidates with a total lack of funds are at a disadvantage—that is true. Any serious candidate, however, will be above that abysmal level.

As a well-prepared contestant, you will already have captured a party or climbed its ranks (a topic that will be further discussed in Part III). You might have made a splash, gained some name recognition, and attracted donations. Once you are at that point, the total gifts you will receive matter marginally. Spending on ads has diminishing returns: after a while, spending more won't matter. More important is where you spend your time and attention; that is where you can make a massive difference compared to the competition.

That money plays a small role can be empirically verified, and all empirical evidence points towards a lack of influence of money. In the 2016 US presidential race, Hillary Clinton and Donald Trump spent a paltry $2.4 billion. The United States' annual economic output (GDP) in comparison is more than $20 trillion. So the total cost of the campaign for the two major candidates was around 0.01% of GDP, once every four years. The spending in 2016 was lower than in 2012, which in turn was lower than in 2008. Other countries have stricter donation limits and campaign finance regulations. The sums involved there are hence even smaller.

If money truly was a game-changer, don't you think much larger sums would be involved? A couple of billions is pocket change for large worldwide companies. If money made a difference, business and individual donors would donate much more to manipulate the race in their favor. In reality, corporations know this would have little bearing on the outcome, which is why they don't bother spending more.

Vast amounts of data across the world are available on campaign financing. This covers not only presidential races but also parliamentary, state, province, and municipal elections. Researchers have carried many studies on this topic. After crunching the data, almost all research confirms that a candidate's funding matters the least. The economist Steven Levitt, for example, found that *doubling* the campaign spending only gained a candidate *one percentage* point in voter intention. Other studies reached similar conclusions.

But such statistics and data are hastily discarded by the bulk of people. Money is merely a tool, yet it drives many people in their personal lives. They accept, therefore, that money influences political campaigning, despite the available counter-evidence.

Post-election speeches given by the defeated candidates reinforce these beliefs. Losers don't like to say that they failed, that they were unpopular. After such a failure, they, for those reasons, turn on convenient scapegoats like "my opponent commanded more wealth and funds", which sounds better. You, in contrast, dear reader, are smarter than that. You use the available data to guide your actions.

In the 2016 presidential race, Hillary Clinton ($1.4 billion) outspent Donald Trump ($950 million) by a whopping 50%. Nevertheless, she got trounced in the Electoral College vote 227-304.

Even more stunning was the 2018 Brazilian race, according to the data from the Supreme Electoral Court of Brazil. Fernando Haddad spent R$37.5 million (~9.4 million USD) versus less than R$2.5 million (<1 million USD) spent by the eventual winner Jair Bolsanaro. In this case, Bolsanaro won the popular vote by employing 15 times less funds than his main opponent. Let this sink in. Brand those inspirational words in your mind:

Empty pockets never held anyone back.
Only empty heads and empty hearts can do that.
— Norman Vincent Peale

Why campaign spending is overrated

Empirical study demonstrates the low impact of campaign donations on your success. Why is this so? Money matters in many areas of life, so why not here? Let's take a step back and look at the theory. The factors that contribute to the victory of a candidate over another are: (1) Great campaign content such as promising popular policies and playing into people's prejudices; (2) Who you are; (3) the actual transmission of this information to the electorate. If no one hears about you, if your campaign has low visibility, you won't win. Pundits claim it is this third factor where funding matters. For all three elements, though, not money but your human understanding and intelligence matter the most. While commanding vast resources, in theory, helps to get your message across, there are, in practice, many inexpensive ways to achieve it.

Fundamentally, information sharing is cheap. In this digital age, you can share your viewpoints on social media, upload videos, and disseminate your program on your website. That is a low hurdle to cross. During the campaign, the media will interview you, write stories about you, especially if you are already the candidate of an established party (a topic that will be discussed in part III). There will be plenty of opportunities to talk about the dangers the country or humanity faces. You will be able to voice your opinion on that minority you target. You will distribute goodies and fliers with your slogan; this isn't costly.

Mass political campaigning took off with the invention of the printing press. With the use of pamphlets, which are unbound booklets that are cheap to produce and distribute, people spread political ideas and carried out personal attacks. In the seventeenth and eighteenth century, outright pamphlets wars broke out between political opponents. In 1678, hysteria swept through England as pamphlets virulently attacked the catholic pope. Catholics were accused of planning the assassination of the British King. Twenty-two men were as a consequence executed. Parliament passed a bill excluding Catholics from membership of the House. In the aftermath of her acquittal, the catholic Elizabeth Cellier wrote the pamphlet 'Malice Defeated', which gained her renown. This led to renewed political struggle by means of pamphlets between those that supported her and those who didn't. One century later, the French revolutionary Jacques Hébert founded his journal 'Le Père Duchesne'. Therein, he spread his radical views insulting the King and the aristocracy. At the height of the French Revolution, 600,000 copies of his commentaries were printed weekly in France.

Sharing political beliefs was hence already inexpensive in the past centuries. The advent of the internet transformed information sharing, which is now quasi-free. If you have a proper program along the lines set out in previous chapters, you will have the opportunity to broadcast your plans, reach out to voters, and share your vision for the nation.

Gaining name recognition

There are many ways of getting free extra exposure. Even if you have less funding and fewer ads than the opposition, the right plan can more than compensate for that. You can survive on low funds with special tactics. For example, candidates in the past got free TV time when they said unconventional things or offended other contenders. This tactic can pull you far up the race, due to the free advertisement it gives you. Making controversial statements is then worth it. Imperative is that your controversial speech does not offend the majority, but rather turns you into a topic of discussion. People will talk about your statements to their friends, family, colleagues, or on social media. In this way, they give you free publicity. Apply this knowledge to tilt the odds in your favor.

How to generate such controversy? If you follow the instructions from Part I, you have created a popular yet polemical political program for your campaign. Examples are remarks you made on a menace threatening society, or about a minority, or an unrealistic promise you gave. Your usage of pathos is then most rewarding, for plays on emotions grab attention.

Next to an excellent political program, other ways to grab media attention exist. The style in which you communicate plays a significant role. A disruptive campaign is effective in getting the word out and gaining name-recognition.

In the years before he ran for president, Donald J. Trump would often say or tweet outlandish things to gain reputation. For example, he requested at the time that President Barack Obama released his birth certificate. This was, on the one hand, an unusual request. On the other hand, it was not an extreme statement as the constitution requires a presidential candidate to be born within the United States. It was the right mix of not offending the masses or the centrist electorate, while simultaneously grabbing the headline of various media. Donald Trump benefited from the free exposure he got through his eccentric statements and behavior. Look out for such moves that draw attention without making you look like a fool. Once you have reaped fame and notoriety, destiny is in your hand.

Someone like Mark Zuckerberg or Bill Gates, if they would run for president, would be more aided by name-recognition than by their wealth. Gaining fame beforehand can help a lot with spreading your message and building up your credibility. Scientists observed that an average person must have at least five encounters with a candidate before name recognition takes place. This explains the success of actors and comedians in presidential races owing to their celebrity status.

You will further gain free air-time when you are invited to debates. These could be in primaries or debates between the final candidates. Making a splash in the primary debates can go a long way. At first, the candidates with a lot of name recognition will lead the race. But over time and through discussions, lesser-known candidates can establish their name, so that voters become aware of them. In a later chapter, you will read how to behave in a debate to convince the most voters.

In near-all presidential countries, multiple contests between the candidates are held in the electoral campaign. In the French presidential election in 2017, all contenders were invited, even those that polled very low. Five fringe candidates present at that debate scored less than 4% combined. This was not for lack of exposure, but because they held extreme positions or were outright weird. (One of them was a conspiracy theorist, two were far-left pro-communist candidates, and another advocated immediate withdrawal from the EU and the euro.) The content and style of their campaign was unsuited to reach the presidency. You, dear reader, won't blunder like that; you are not playing Don Quixote.

In a nutshell, conventional wisdom overrates campaign spending and underrates name recognition. If you aren't so well known yet 6 months before the election, money will be of little help. And if your name and face is unfamiliar to the public 18 months before the election, ways exist to overcome the disadvantage of possessing few funds.

*

Along with all the Dos in previous paragraphs, there a couple of Don'ts. Even if, at one point in time, you are low on cash, then hang on to the race. Realize that money is not the most important factor for winning. Resigning early is more than a character flaw—it is an error. Once you start pulling ahead in the polls, more people will donate to your cause. Tides can turn, and over time more donations will stream to your war chest. In a joke of destiny, money does not cause winning, but being ahead in the race will attract money.

One more Don't is cheating the electoral finance law. Worse than a crime, it is a mistake. It is a mistake because you run a high risk of being jailed and have your political career shattered, yet the reward from cheating is low. Some candidates, for a little money that wouldn't have impacted their election odds, thus lost all. Cases of this blunder abound. For example, in 2014, the Bygmalion Scandal came to light in France. The major center-right party UMP was accused of making fictitious invoices to circumvent campaign spending limits. The leader of that party, Jean François Copé, was forced to step down and saw his political ambitions squashed. Don't throw this advice to the wind.

Raise money

Let's turn to the details of campaign finance. It is not an easy task to write a general approach to it since the laws regulating it differ a lot by country. There might be donation limits per person. In France, the law caps the amount of individual donations at 7500 euros per year for a party, and 4600 euros for a candidate's campaign. In the United States, the constitutional court judged on this topic in the landmark case (Citizens United). In that case, it considered that individuals and companies have an almost limitless right to donate and support electoral campaigns. The judges ruled that the free speech enshrined in the First Amendment of the Constitution of the United States grants this.

Different ways of raising money for your cause exist:
(1) donations to your candidacy;
(2) or action groups that spend money to support your campaign;
(3) or the treasury of the political party that you have captured, or whose ranks you climbed.
Your party will support your campaign with the contributions of all party members. (More on that in Part III.)

When eliciting donations, pretend each donation counts. Make the donor feel like they are making a difference. This is untrue; however, the donor needs to feel psychological gratification when handing you over his or her money.

The Obama campaign in 2008 demonstrated the strength of millions of small donors. Through an at the time innovative internet campaign, Obama was able to attract many small donations: 90 percent of all gifts came from people donating $100 or less, and 40 percent from donors who gave $25 or less. While the average donation was low, the number of contributors more than compensated that.

Where to spend money

On the spending side, a well-advised candidate spends the money in the right places. A big war chest without the right management serves no purpose. Campaign spending is divided into four categories.

Advertising

Ads should end up being the major expense of your campaign. Campaign ads inform voters that you exist and that you are a viable alternative to the other candidates. These comprise of ads on television, radio, on billboards, or online.

Direct mail is the printing of booklets and their distribution through the post. It is the traditional method of transmitting your political project. It still has its place, but you shouldn't send booklets to every house. You can save money on this category if you can target the houses or key neighborhoods where it will have the most impact.

In the next chapter, I analyze the impact of technology. New developments allow for much more efficient, targeted advertising.

Events and Travels

Part of your campaign will consist of events were you give speeches and encounter your base. These expenses can add up if the country is large. Some candidates are traveling in private jets and stay at expensive hotels. This makes no sense; instead, make the small upfront sacrifice for the long term gain by staying in a cheaper hotel. There is also no need to bring over a huge team.

In future elections, physically traveling to an event will be replaced by 3D holograms. Instead of reaching a couple of thousands assembled at a spot, you can speak and interact virtually with millions. Physically meeting is, however, still a different feeling, especially on an emotional level. When persons physically meet you and dialogue with you, they will take selfies, share pictures with friends, and talk about you to their colleagues. They will turn into free advertisers for you. The thrill—the pathos, as described in the first chapter—of encountering a major candidate for presidency in real life should not be underestimated.

Research and Strategy

Many undervalue research on voter intention. An early start to your campaign allows you to poll the people, either by directly talking to them or hiring a survey company. Polling is most helpful; do it often and well. Survey research is your friend. As already written before, promising what the population wants has to be an integral part of your campaign. Carry out an intelligent analysis of the situation at hand. You can lever it afterward in your overall strategy, your campaign content, your style, and your usage of technology and ads.

Payroll

Payroll is to pay for all those employed in your campaign. You need a competent and skilled central team to advise you, and to run the basic aspects of your campaign. An organization of people has a higher working capacity and allows for specialization. That increases productivity because each individual is or becomes an expert in one domain. The team can help determine your plan, discover weaknesses that are in your blind spot, and execute your campaign strategy. Maintain a team of experts so that all domains are covered.

It is recommended to keep payroll spending at a somewhat modest 10-15% of your campaign budget. Carry out a lean campaign; it is not a job program. It is better to collaborate with a small, focused team than a large, unwieldy group where miscommunication thrives. If a group gets too large (> 50-100 persons), overhead is required to steer internal communication and strategy. Wiser is to supplement a core team with self-organized volunteers that don't cost money.

In the past, candidates would spend more on ground, local teams. The proximity of such teams helped them build trust with locals and get a better read on the electorate. But—especially with modern day technology—it is cheaper to connect to large parts of the electorate through ads. It is, therefore, no hazard that recent winners focused less on ground teams, and more on overarching strategy, polling, and online ads (notably Donald Trump's campaign in 2016). The US Federal Election Commission filings indicate that Hillary Clinton massively outspent Donald Trump on staff payroll, an approach that did not bear fruits.

*

In summary, don't be discouraged if you have low funding, for it hardly matters anyway. Generating controversy instead, to remain in traditional and social media's attention, can go a long way. On the spending side, the quality of your message and how you communicate are more important than the quantity of ads. How to achieve this quality is addressed in the next chapters.

Chapter 6
Take advantage of technology

All tools have intrinsic politics,
and technology is the tool of now
— Godfrey Reggio

The flow of information is faster and cheaper today than it has ever been. When disseminating your message, all research shows that communication technologies matter the most. Mastering them is the key to success. A well-prepared candidate has to remain on top of all the latest trends in telecommunication.

History is strewn by dark horses clutching the presidency employing new media. When the radio gained traction in the 1930s, for illustration, the Nazis mastered this new communication device and ushered in a new era. They managed to spread their message through it, while other political factions made no use of the nascent media platform. The other parties were left in the dust.

At the same time, in the USA, Franklin D. Roosevelt (four times elected president) addressed the electorate through evening talks on the radio. These were his famous Fireside Chats, where he would promote in an informal manner his policy. For the first time in history, a large segment of the population could listen directly to the president or to a candidate. They were not solely relying anymore on the reporting of the press.

It is no surprise that contemporary candidates who adapted to the advent of social media, scored big in recent years. Once you are trending on Twitter and have amassed many followers, what does money matter? It is drawing eyeballs that count so that you can share your program and proposals and drown out your opponents' attempts at doing the same. With the emergence of social media as an alternative channel, you can even afford poor relations with traditional media. When the press starts bashing you, you can circumvent them by directly addressing your followers through social media.

Technology and disinformation

In the Nigerian 2019 election, those in power had more money to invest in their campaign and controlled the government-aligned radio. The opposition had less airtime and was victim of some fake news. Propaganda and disinformation has always existed in communist and Third World countries. Still, social media have given both a new life and reach, even in well-established European and American democracies.

To counter disinformation, the Nigerian opposition organized itself with the help of WhatsApp groups. This smartphone app allows groups of up to 256 members. The central command would send a message in a WhatsApp group to counter the fake news spread by its opponents. Members of this group would share it in turn with other local groups, and these groups would do the same in turn. This made it possible to spread messages across tens of thousands of individuals with the click of a button.

In the past, it was challenging to counteract disinformation spread by the government. Technology has thus leveled the playing field. The emergence of mass media has enabled the use of propaganda and counter-propaganda techniques on a societal scale. Social media increase your reach in a way that expensive advertising or direct mail can't.

The word 'propaganda' has over the 20th century acquired a negative connotation. This text won't delve in morals, as already many other individuals lecture us about what is good and what is evil. Realpolitik and a pragmatic mindset guide candidates who wish to win.

You and your opponents might be accused of practicing propaganda. Some propaganda is, however, part of a healthy political discourse; a little misinformation or disinformation is part of political warfare. It is desirable that you can grab people's attention. That way, they will be more informed and find out about your person and other contestants. Employ such pragmatic methods to ensure you don't draw the shortest straw.

Personalized ads

As Nigeria's case illustrates: you have to remain on the lookout for breakthroughs in the means of communication. Use your campaign funds wisely by leveraging the latest trends in technology. Don't spend much on TV ads, direct mail, or billboards. Knocking on every door is very inefficient and costs a lot of time. Instead of spending money through the old channels, spend on digital ads.

In most countries, the practice of online ads for political campaigning hasn't fully caught on yet. In the 2019 general election in Flanders, the extreme right Vlaams Belang party spent as much on online ads as all the other parties combined. It relied upon Facebook ads as its core marketing strategy. In the 2014 election, it scored only 5.8%. In 2019 though, it more than tripled its score to 18.5%. It came as a total surprise as, although the polls gave them some gains, this order of magnitude was unexpected. Other far-right parties had been on the decline in Europe after the migrant stream from 2015 ebbed away. Vlaams Belang bombarded voters with ads, targeting the right segments of the electorate susceptible to flip. Other parties remained muted on social media, relying instead on traditional channels. In a competitive political landscape, parties that don't adapt to technology die.

Online advertisement is not only cheap, but also allows for targeting specific voters. TV ads are blunt tools since they reach everyone with the same message. Digital ads enable you to focus on swing voters. You can personalize the message. They allow sending messages based on age, gender, interests, friends, and location of the viewer (and much more…). TV ads are like a saw; digital ads are like a scalpel.

You can, for example, mention you want to legalize marijuana when the viewer is young. Or decrease the VAT (Value Added Tax) on tampons when addressing women. Or talk about the rising sea levels when the viewer lives on the coast. You have, of course, used part of your campaign spending for polling what policy polls best with which group. Your campaign should, though, keep an overall coherence. The trick is to highlight distinct parts of your program to different viewers.

How to optimize personalized ads

Online ads have many qualities that enable sophisticated statistics. Since they are cheap and easy to run for a short while, it is possible to run many experiments. One simple trick is called **"A/B testing"**, a standard tool in marketing which some political parties remain ignorant of. This consists of displaying two alternative messages to different users at random. To one group, you show your ad "A". To the second group, you show your alternative message "B". The difference between A and B could be some words, or the color of your tie, or something more substantial. After a short while, you will be able to gather statistics on all those who saw the two versions of the message. For example, you can compare your two invitations to explore your program based on how many interacted with it. You can so know which generates the most clicks and is, therefore, the most effective version. If the experiment shows that "B" elicits more user interaction, you can stop running ad "A".

Because of the massive traffic on the internet, you can often run such experiments every hour, or sometimes even shorter timeframes. Let the data drive you. Your online ad strategy that way evolves and becomes more effective by the hour. It is not rare for a well-organized campaign to run one billion targeted digital adverts. These go mostly via Facebook and other online websites. By running many different versions of ads (version "A", "B", ...), your campaign can test which ones work the best. Drop the less effective and reinforced the most effective in a constant iterative process. And so hone your message in a scientific way.

"A/B testing" is not hard and does not require profound knowledge of mathematics or statistics. All you need to do is to prepare two ads, and display randomly one at the time, and count up how many clicked on them. With this technique, newspapers have discovered that fear-based articles are more often read than others, and have polished—to their benefit—the click-baiting-headline approach.

There are more advanced statistical methods, such as **machine learning**, which you should incorporate into your marketing. Massive datasets, as well as more powerful computers, nowadays allow finding hidden relations in data. The data could come from social media, your online ads, internet crawling, online fundraising, and bought from private sources.

Based on a series of factors about the individual and the ads shown to them, machine learning can predict who will donate to your campaign, or what the voting intention of an individual is. While A/B testing allows you to improve your online campaign, machine learning enables truly targeted marketing. For illustration, a statistical model based on massive datasets can predict who is most likely to donate and if the sum will be large. It might predict that you should show a specific message eliciting donations to 40-45-year-old married women who recently went to your website. Or the model could track undecided voters. Individuals who have publicized their allegiance are unlikely to switch. But you can still sway the undecided voters to your side. It is them foremost you should bombard with information.

The Vote Leave campaign in the UK Brexit so built the 'Voter Intention Collection System', which was an application predicting voting intentions of British citizens. It made use of massive datasets and machine learning.

Computer scientists, physicists, and mathematicians are supplanting political analysts and marketing specialists. These latter ones rarely base themselves on data. Instead, they invoke "expert judgment" in their analyses and recite mantras. The former ones apply the scientific method to big data and so outperform traditional experts; this is called data science.

Traditional advertising eschews data. This allows them to make exaggerated statements about the effectiveness of their campaigns, because their claims are unverifiable. Thus they base entire strategies on a set of old dogmas. In contrast, modern advertising embraces data and transparency. For data enables a culture of rational, scientific decision making, and overcoming human biases and other false beliefs.

Keep track of voter intention

It is wise to keep a list of persons that are likely to vote for you. They might have donated, subscribed to your newsletter, or machine learning indicates they are in your favor. Although there is no need to convince them anymore, you should still send them the message to remind them to vote. Most countries don't have mandatory voting. Therefore, part of your campaign is about getting your supporters to the polling booth. Accomplish this via emails or robocalls.

Also, machine learning can also indicate if someone has no interest in politics whatsoever. Avoid spending money on politically apathetic people.

People that don't sympathize with your cause should, of course, not be reminded about going to vote. If they are in the opponent's camp, then don't waste money on them. But, if they only somewhat lean towards your rival, then target them with negative ads. By digging up political dirt about your opponents, their supporters become disgusted with their candidates and don't go voting at all.

*

That is what campaigns are for: to bring information to the otherwise uninformed population. That is why you spend money. It is recommended you master the latest media trends and the telecommunication sector. You should have a grasp of statistics too. Hire people on your team to fill gaps in your knowledge. Have no doubts: your opponents will attempt to win by all means. A noble mind, bravery, or charitableness won't win the election, but cleverness and cunning will. Apply any (sophisticated) method at hand to sway citizens.

While your voters are somewhat irrational, you are not. You shall base your campaign strategy on data. And, assisted by your team funded by your campaign, you will apply the scientific method to optimize your path to victory.

*

Losers that don't take advantage of technology go extinct on the political scene. This is a natural consequence of the laws of the universe. A look at the famous first televised debate ever in the 1960 United States presidential election demonstrates this once more.

At the time, television was still a novelty. On a black and white screen, 80 million people watched the duel between the two major candidates: John F. Kennedy versus Richard Nixon. JFK had vast experience with television because his father had invested in Hollywood and ran film studios. His father would involve him in the business so that the son would master the filming process. This aided him in his later political career.

In the debate between the presidential candidates, Nixon got smashed. His appearance on television was terrible. He was sweaty, seemed pale and ill, and his eyes didn't focus on the camera. JFK, in contrast, young and charismatic, understood television. He addressed the audience by looking at the camera and had makeup applied. Most listeners on the radio declared Nixon the winner of the clash, but JFK swayed those that watched via television. JFK's excellent understanding of new technologies led to his victory. After the debate, polls showed JFK, who before had been polling behind, swung to a narrow lead. He went on to win the neck-to-neck race with 49.72% of the vote to Nixon's 49.55%.

*

It is surprising how campaigns are won or lost based on the one-sided understanding of technology. It bears no doubt that future innovations will impact elections. In the present and near future, employ targeted ads instead of costly and broad approaches like TV ads and direct mailing. Remain on the lookout for progress made in the field of information and communication; you have to be information savvy. I can't foresee all the developments in the future of this area. I leave it up to the reader to adapt the knowledge and instructions here provided to the times ahead.

Chapter 7
Style your communication

*A reliable way to make people believe in falsehoods is frequent
repetition,
because familiarity is not easily distinguished from truth
— Daniel Kahneman*

Logical arguments (logos) in favor of your policies persuade few.
People will not judge you on reason, plans, or results. It is rather
the emotions you evoke and the passions on which you play that
matter. Your hyperbolic rhetoric needs to resonate with the deep-
felt sentiments of the voters.

You should have by now a good program in place, as
discussed in Part I:

(1) Your plans are popular;

(2) You talk about an imminent danger; and

(3) You have provided for a scapegoat for the country's woes.

In previous chapter we've looked at the means of communications.
Now, apply expert communication tricks and techniques to
formulate your message and get it across. In this endeavor, pathos
is once more the most compelling approach. This is because
emotions enhance memory of and attention to your message.

Let's analyze how you should style and structure your
communication for maximal effect.

Repetition

An important learning from the advertisement industry is that repetition works. People need to see you a few times before they start remembering you as a candidate. Scientists have studied this phenomenon and display it in what is called 'forgetting curves'.

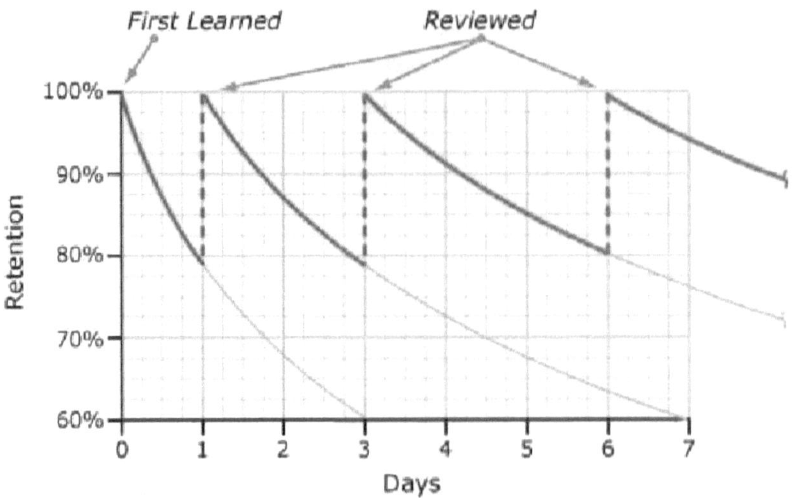

A forgetting curve - how information is retained over time

Let's inspect the decline of memory retention in time. It has been observed that humans tend to halve their memory of newly learned knowledge in a matter of days. Thankfully, repetition is potent. When reviewing previously learned material, it is remembered much longer. This is also true for learning at school: children remember subject matter much better when they have repeated it a couple of times. All studies have observed the power of repetition.

Armed with this knowledge, reiterate your political message so that it buries itself in the unconsciousness of the listener or viewer. And when you state your message again, the audience will instinctively feel it is true. This effect has been studied by psychologist such as the renowned Daniel Kahneman. Repetition is, therefore, an intelligent procedure to persuade voters of your ideas and plans.

Exploit repetition tactics not only to highlight the grave dangers the country faces, but also for slandering opponents. Donald Trump, serving President of the USA, is a master of this trick. He nicknamed opponents, notably 'crooked Hillary' after her email controversy. The constant repetition of the nickname in debates, speeches, and ads, exerted a strong subconscious influence on voters' minds. Many disagreed with the nickname at first. But, when he reiterated it again and again, people's opinions shifted under the cumulative pressure of each attack. And so, even Hillary voters ended up conceding that she was not clean. In this fashion, Trump swayed swing voters in 2016 to abstain from voting for Hillary Clinton.

A favorite of those advocating vigorous policies to fight climate change is pointing at extreme weather events. Average temperatures don't grab headlines as much. It is much more useful to repeat the climate change mantra when a heatwave or tropical cyclone hits. The intensity of such events marks people's minds. The coverage in the media determines how people judge the importance of an issue—this is also called the availability bias. The constant attention spent on the topic then causes the public to believe the danger is real.

In summary, repetition is a simple but effective marketing trick that should be part of your arsenal.

Keep it simple

Next to repetition, you should also keep your message uncomplicated. Wield anecdotes instead of statistics when you address the people. You have to reach 99% of the voters. The intelligent people will understand you are simplifying your speech to reach a broader segment of the population. Ban statistics from your discourse; it bores people and they are bad at it. A thoughtful cost-benefit analysis, weighing probabilities, or even mentioning numbers will cause public apathy. In 2004 John Kerry, on the topic of terrorism, talked with numbers (counting terrorism and traffic casualties), instead of appealing to emotions. That unfortunate statement earned him a lot of criticism. Between data and drama, go for drama.

When communicating, attempt to concentrate your message in five to seven points. Studies have shown that most humans can only retain seven items in their mind. The social scientist Miller already discovered in 1956 that humans have limits on their capacity for processing information. Adults have between 5 and 9 'slots' in their short-term memory. Each slot can store an item so that it can be recalled later. Your campaign's main talking points should, hence, consist of five to at most seven policy plans. People anyway won't remember more than that.

Nonetheless, don't discard an exhaustive 100-point political program immediately. It can provide details to the interested without interfering with your communication with the rest of the electorate. You can also steal voters from adjacent parties by taking over some of the other contestants' policy proposals. A 100-point program can also come in handy if you wish to ally with other parties. You can so build a broad coalition and keep your allies happy by burying some of their pet projects in your 100-points. (If you will implement all 100 and remain faithful to your partners is a question you can deal later with.) Some people like that you have so many plans; you will seem prepared for everything. However, your 100-point program will only be found on your website. When you talk on television, on the radio, before an audience, you will be succinct and highlight no more than five to seven main points. People can't handle more.

Multi-level messaging

A message often has a literal and an underlying part. Understanding the hidden or implied message requires knowledge of the cultural and historical background. Foreigners or different subgroups will miss this, so you can apply this to your advantage without them realizing. The idea is as follows: your literal message appeals to the masses and seems innocent, but the underlying isn't. It is instead meant to send a message and please a subgroup of people. For illustration, Barack Obama would make Afro-American moves. The white electorate would be oblivious for it, whereas the Afro-Americans understood the secret message: Obama signaled he was one of them.

And Ronald Reagan, in his winning run in 1980, would often appeal to decentralization and state rights. How much power the federal government holds, and how much is left to the states or provinces seems like a reasonable topic for a candidate to bring up. On the surface, this is in a federal country like the USA a valid subject for debate. Yet state rights also refer to the reconstruction period 110 years before. In those times, white Southerners were legally able to reduce black turnout in elections with the help of poll taxes. The message of state rights did not fall in deaf ears: white Southerners voted en masse for Reagan. This multilevel messaging is also called dog-whistling. Dogs can hear the frequencies of a whistle that humans can't. These type of coded messages are effective in gaining and retaining new groups of supporters, yet avoid alienating the existing ones.

The meaning of certain concepts can also be obscured by frequent and deliberate misuse. An example is the word 'neo-liberalism', which politicians misused so often it has lost all meaning. Both left and right-wing in Europe and Latin-America attack this ideology, and no one defends it. The literal meaning of a speech becomes obfuscated because each assumes a different underlying message. Neo-liberalism has become a straw-man associated with negative feelings. Language can, in this way, corrupt thoughts.

Another hornet's nest in Europe is the topic of Israel. Be careful not to offend any side since you will need all the support you can get to win. If you declare an act of the Israeli government as illegal, many won't fail to recognize the underlying message. Even if you didn't mean it like that, plenty would understand you think the state of Israel itself is illegitimate. Navigate those mined waters with great care, as so many things can be misunderstood. Jeremy Corbyn, a former leader of the British Labour Party, provided his opponents ample material for criticism—which contributed to his defeat in the 2019 UK election. He among others appeared on Iranian TV criticizing specific actions of Israel, and invited ''friends from the Hamas.'' Don't make the unforced error to bring this topic up.

Hyperbolic rhetoric

You will as well make frequent use of hyperboles. Your bold vision, accompanied by flowery words, will arouse the public. And your enthusiastic supporters will follow every word and act of yours and hang at your lips. People want a vision; they long for it. Promise them Utopia, or proclaim impending Doom. For the electorate wants you to sell them a dream. All victorious candidates spiced up their program and behaved as showmen. Mario Cuomo, multiple times Governor of the State of New York, laconically remarked that ''You campaign in poetry. You govern in prose.'' Poetry is necessary to get your message across.

Because of incessant lies and exaggerations of past candidates, it is, at times, challenging to break out. In today's crowded political competitions, it is hard to cut through the noise. This is why the hyperbole is your best friend. Too many politicians have come out against higher taxes, yet done nothing once elected. That is why, to stand out in the crowd, you have to come with over the top statements. It is a universal, natural law of campaigning.

For example, suppose you believe that taxes are too high and hamper economic growth. Then generate controversy like this: ''We will lower taxes so much, you won't even know what to do with all this money.'' If someone contests this as absurd, double down and repeat loudly, because it will boost your credibility. This expressive language signals voters that you are not like the others. You are not going to produce cosmetic changes. You are the real deal. You mean business. Of course, you won't literally halve taxes, but you will at least create drastic changes.

When you want to reform the institutions, then say: ''Politics is too serious of a matter to be left to politicians.'' That is a strong statement. It hits a populists cord, yet also echoes a famous phrase from the well-respected prime minister of France during World War I (''War is too serious to be left to generals''—Clemenceau).

If you run with this phrase in France, you would catch two fishes with one bait.

Donald J. Trump's best line from the 2016 election was without doubt: "We're going to build a wall and Mexico is going to pay [for it]." Across the world, people remarked Trump was dumb—or at least his supporters. In their view, the statement was absurd. But this wasn't true. Trump's core supporters did understand that Mexico wouldn't pay for it. As for Trump, his comment was pure genius, because it set him apart from all those other politicians who, in the past, took mere superficial and cosmetic action against (illegal) immigration. It was all about signaling, showing that he was not like the other contenders. It was a home run and gained a lot of free media attention to boot. Bold statements on emotionally sensitive topics are necessary to go viral.

What would happen if instead of such bold and colorful proposals, you make a smaller, realistic promise? Voters will think your halfhearted pledge will never come to fruition, as happened so often in the past election cycles. Or worse: they won't even hear about you. (Any publicity is good publicity.) This why past politicians declared "War on Terrorism" and "War on Drugs". These exaggerated statements ensured the population believed these politicians would for a change truly do something useful.

How to make policy proposals sound good

If you want to persuade an audience, you need to employ the right words to frame your opinion and proposed policies. When addressing them, don't shy away from euphemisms. Don't state: "I'm going to raise taxes and spend more of it on education."

That is how a technocrat would frame it, not a savvy candidate. And on top of that, don't talk about taxes, people hate them unless you are going to lower them. Instead, pimp your message and say: ''I am not going to leave any child behind.'' It is about pathos, remember? Fighting for children, and against abandonment—these are the right pictures to evoke. For who is against leaving no child behind? By stating your policies in this manner, opposition to them will be hard. People will nod their heads when they hear you because the opposite statement is so despicable and repulsive.

All your plans should sound attractive; create a list of all your positions and proposals from Part I and reformulate them in this way. You are going to help, protect, or defend the people, children, veterans, or nature. You are for the social good, whatever that is supposed to mean. Appeal to broad principles everyone can get behind. Values such as family, patriotism, fairness, freedom are excellent examples that almost all cherish. Children are particularly effective as a tool in political campaigning. For illustration, George Bush, in the US election in 2000, called his educational reform plan ''Leave no Child Behind.''

Moreover, instead of saying ''stop trading with other nations,'' say ''buy local'' and so appeal to their economic patriotism. And say: ''everyone needs to contribute fairly.'' This is, of course, meaningless for it all depends on what you mean with fair and how you will implement it. But that is how winning works. And if a majority in the polls backs on of your proposals, say ''the majority supports me.'' If there is no clear majority, claim ''the silent majority supports me.''

In addition, use buzzwords but avoid those that have been too popular in recent times. You want to use those that are on the rise.

Overuse of buzzwords from the past election cycle makes you look old and insincere.

Some call these communication techniques mass manipulation or propaganda; a savvy candidate calls it public relations. Propaganda is the same, but the word acquired negative connotations since Dr. Goebbels headed the Ministry of Propaganda in Nazi Germany. You should always have some experts in public relations within your staff. It is amazing how you, with extensive propaganda, can lead people to believe anything.

Negative Ads

Furthermore, discredit your opponents with attacking ads. Negative advertisements will sow doubt in the electorate. After all, where there is smoke, there is fire. You and your campaign team have to attack the wickedness and corrupt personae of your opponents. Parts of the public can thus be swayed to vote for you, or to abstain from voting for your opponents. An attack on your rivals' personality is one of the best styles of persuasion based on ethos. Such techniques based on someone's character play in presidential campaigns an out-sized role compared to rational arguments.

A great and infamous historical case is from the 1988 US presidential campaign. In an ad, George H.W. Bush attacked his opponent Dukakis on crime and the death penalty, which the latter wanted to abolish. ''Dukakis allowed murderers weekend passes. One condemned prisoner fled during his weekend pass. During his flight, he kidnapped a couple, stabbing and raping them.'' That was an excellent application of an anecdote to instill fear in the minds of the electorate. Bush's campaign repeated the ad over and over again. Voters were not able to get this image out of their heads, of Dukakis as weak and soft on crime.

Multiple 1988 campaign ads, containing negative messages about opponents accompanied by fear-evoking music and images, exerted a strong influence on voters. Dukakis, till the ad aired, led by a wide margin. This well-delivered attack allowed George H.W. Bush to come from 10 points behind in the polls.

Negative advertising works well. Therefore, have your team (that you finance with the money you raised) produce and broadcast ads where you highlight the weaknesses and mistakes of another contender. This will blacken his or her image. The case mentioned above serves as a template of practical attack politics.

Why are negative ads potent? The issue is that voters don't pay much attention to typical campaign ads. The less provocative positive ads fade away over time. They need to be repeated to be effective, which costs a lot of money. Negative ads, on the contrary, captivate the audience. The attacking ads pass on your message to the public more effectively since negative sentiments stick. The human brain is rigged in such a way we recall negative aspects better than positive aspects.

Adopt such techniques to undermine your opponent's credibility and destroy their reputation. It might generate an outcry of your rivals in countries where this tactic isn't widespread yet. However, attack ads provide usable information about other candidates, and thus voters won't punish you.

Furthermore, it is often easier to conceive a fine-tuned attack on the contender's flaws than invent your own positive message. You should have someone on your staff dig into the other candidates' past to find weaknesses or scandals you can exploit.

With the findings, put doubt in the mind of voters who would otherwise vote for your opponent.

In a parliamentary democracy with proportional representation, even if you only obtain 5% of the vote, you still gain seats. If you can carve out a small part of the electorate, this is sufficient. You might later even participate in government by allying with other parties. (So don't alienate them too much beforehand.)

But coming up with a positive message that attracts a fraction of the electorate, let's say farmers or independents, won't win the majority over to you. In presidential systems, it is all or nothing; you win or you lose. Either your opponent or you that become president, with all the power this entails. This requires you to attack other contestants as much as you build up your own candidacy. For that reason, polarization is the natural law of presidential systems.

Tell a story

A message can get across more readily if spun into a story. Tell a story about some ordinary person you met, about the challenge he or she faced. With this story, which is inspired by a true anecdote, you will make a statement about your values.

The next level of this tactic is to narrate a story from your own life. How you were raised by your poor parents, single grandmother, etcetera, but overcame the odds because of your belief in certain values. This type of storytelling, either in a speech or in a debate, seems to work particularly well with the US public; they are gullible and love this trope. Therefore, most examples come from the USA.

The archetype in modern history is, without a doubt, Barack Obama's 2004 DNC keynote speech. Therein, he introduced himself and delineated his values by telling about his parents and grandparents. He weaved his personal story with American history by referencing the Great Depression, The Second World War, the GI Bill, and how this impacted his family. And he employed the classical cliché of the American Dream. (''My presence on this stage is pretty unlikely. My father was a foreign student.'') This iconic speech catapulted an unnoticed senator of Illinois to the national stage and later to the White House. The immigrant-dream-narrative is a good leitmotif in the USA. All Americans (apart from a small group of natives) namely descent from immigrants.

Each country has its images, its symbols, its history, its tropes. Capitalize on them, as Obama did. Kamala Harris, after the first 2020 Democratic primary debate, skyrocketed in the polls. She broke out by attacking Joe Biden on the topic of racism. She did this with a mere three lines on the subject of busing, which marked the end of the separation of black and white children in US schools. ''There was a little girl in California who was part of the second class to integrate her public schools. She was bused to school every day. That little girl was me.'' Overnight with these simple three lines, she surged ten percentage points in the polls. In debates, a topic that I will discuss in more details later on in Part IV, it is about stating who you are and what you stand for. It is a prime chance to tell your story. Her campaign later petered out because her name recognition wasn't high and she didn't generate enough controversy to feature regularly on the front page of the media. This kept her out of the news while adversaries filled the void.

In a very similar fashion, Oprah Winfrey made a stunning speech when receiving an award at the 2018 Golden Globes. In her address, she used a single crime case during the Jim Crow era, to make a stand against racism. Next, she vividly recounted the fate of her grandmother, to underline the importance of government-sponsored healthcare. Oprah alongside delivered a passionate defense of women, in particular in light of the MeToo affair. Oprah was already a celebrity and benefited from wide name recognition in the USA. Her speech raised emotions; many voices thereafter asked her to run for president. Although she later declined, it shows the power of storytelling.

Science now also backs the finding that humans like stories. In experiments, neuroscientists observed that *compelling* narratives cause oxytocin release in the human brain. Oxytocin is a hormone that boosts our feelings of trust and compassion. It regulates our attitudes, beliefs, and behaviors. As a candidate, you can hence gain the trust of the people with a well-told character-driven story.

Inception

In all of your communication, it is advised to avoid too overt propaganda. There will always be an inherent distrust of politicians and political advertisements. Even companies shy away from too direct, blatant ads. Imagine for a moment the marketing department of a corporation selling eggs. It runs an ad ''Our eggs are the best!'' Do you think the public will believe it? No, of course not. Such a head-on appeal doesn't work well because it is too blunt and direct.

Much smarter is a subtler message like ''Doctors say eggs are healthy.'' This is an appeal to authority. Most people find doctors trustworthy and will then connect the dots. They will buy the eggs and be persuaded it was their idea. In reality, you have incepted the idea in their mind.

Addressing crowds

One last point is to adapt to the size of the public and to the medium. Are you talking to a small group of donors? Are you speaking to the entire nation through the television? Are you standing in front of a massive crowd at a rally? When addressing crowds, a set of rules have to be kept in mind. You must appeal to the masses. This is not a small group of scientifically trained intelligentsia. Target their emotions, play on pathos, and galvanize them. Adopt rather simple and straightforward language and use at most one or two uncomplicated metaphors.

Three distinct psychological further affect the crowd. First: in a large group, an individual is merely an anonymous person. Anonymity changes human behavior. It creates a feeling of invincibility because it is unlikely any offender will be punished. That causes them to lose civility. It is no hazard the anonymity in internet begets harsh or hateful statements. Second: strong emotions trigger similar feelings in other people. When a person smiles, you are more likely to smile. When a person yawns, you also feel like yawning. In a crowd, emotional contagion amplifies joy, anger, and frenzy. Third: the mass needs a leader. It realizes it needs to be coordinated. They are like soldiers marching as dictated by their officer, obeying even if only to avoid collision. It is up to you to direct the otherwise inarticulate action of the mob. Armed with this knowledge, the astute leader who you aspire to be will tailor his or her speech to fire up the crowds.

Over the past pages, I have detailed how you should style and structure your communication for maximal effect. With the help of those techniques, you will disseminate your political program and convert people to your cause.

Chapter 8
Create a good slogan

One day, a talented lass or fellow,
a special one with face of yellow,
will find the piece of resistance,
from it's hiding refuge underground,
and with a noble army at the helm,
this Master-builder will thwart the kragle and save the realm,
and become the greatest, most interesting person of all times,
and all of it is true because it rhymes.
— Prophet Vitruvius, The Lego Movie (2014)

A slogan is a key element when publicizing your political manifesto. The word ''slogan'' originates from Scottish Gaelic and means ''battle-cry''. In modern-day language, the meaning has shifted: it is a catchy phrase or series of words used for branding.

Why a slogan

Slogans are used both by corporations and by political campaigns. Similar to a company, your electoral campaign should have one as well. Research has shown that they catch attention, help convey messages, and build trust.

People don't vote because they expect that their *single* vote will matter in a nation of millions. They don't vote because in the belief their *single* vote will affect policy. It is mathematically so unlikely that it would be irrational to hold such beliefs. Individuals intuitively understand this. And in the improbable case that an election ends up 50-50% and you would cast the deciding vote, the election result would anyway be contested and redone. A single vote won't change the country's course, which is why a voter cares less about your program than a four-word slogan. Voters seek to express themselves, not because anyone will be listening in the booth, but because it is an innate pleasure of man to boo or cheer on others.

Voting is like cheering in a soccer match; it won't change the outcome, yet everyone does it. People pay for sports games since it is amusing and diverting. For the same reason, people go vote not because it will personally benefit them, but because it entertains them.

You can always find someone else to write your program. You should only set some high-level direction (right, center, left, populist, etcetera) that suits your needs. Leave the details to your staff. But pay careful attention to your slogans and put effort into them, for they allow you to convey your whole program at once. What thrills supporters of a sports team are its colors (your catchphrase) and its personalities (you). The detailed content does not. Recall that, not logos, but pathos wins presidential elections.

Brevity is wit

The best argument against democracy is a five-minute conversation with the average voter, Winston Churchill said. A good slogan, though, should convince a voter not in 5 minutes but in a mere 5 seconds. Make it easy to remember, concise, and appealing to the public.

Keep your slogan succinct. Obama, in his victorious presidential campaign in 2008, adopted the slogan ''Change We Can Believe In.'' But that was already too long and complex. When his supporters started chanting ''Yes We Can,'' Obama's campaign team took it over. That was a superb move as ''Yes We Can'' is a simpler and more condensed form of the former (and was actually invented by the National Scottish Party). As a rule of thumb, your slogan should not exceed four words. A longer motto can work, on condition that you apply literary tricks to help to remember it.

It is desirable that your rallying cry rhymes because it is then easier to remember. As said before, even a five-word catchphrase can be too long to recall. Also, many voters consider rhymes to be 'smart' and 'true'—as lampshaded in the opening quote of this chapter.

Nobel Prize winner Daniel Kahneman, observed in his research that humans suffer from several cognitive biases. In his book 'Thinking Slow and Fast' he reports that the easier it is to recall a message, the more likely we perceive and accept it as true. Keep, therefore, your slogan straightforward and memorable. Humans, it seems, are quite gullible when massaged with the right techniques.

A good, rhyming case is the catchphrase ''No Taxation without Representation,'' created by American revolutionaries. And the motto of the French Revolution: ''Liberty, Equality, Fraternity.'' Or the attacking message ''In Your Guts, You Know He's Nuts,'' which was used by L.B. Johnson in his campaign against B. Goldwater in 1964. Much like a song chorus or a company jingle that gets stuck in your head, a fine slogan needs to have a rhythm or sound that rolls off the tongue that makes it instantly recognizable.

In literature and especially poetry, certain techniques are often used. These are called rhetorical or stylistic devices. Clever usage of sound and structure of a language can not only result in great poetry, but also in powerful slogans.

A classical stylistic device is the alliteration, where one repeats the same letter or sound within nearby words. It was already well known in ancient classical times; the Roman orator and politician Cicero was a fond user of this rhetorical device. This device is even more suited to modern times, as we live in an era of soundbites and sharing short messages on social media. It has become more powerful than ever before. The British conservatives, for example, ran with ''*S*trong and *S*table Leadership.'' The usage of such devices wins minds. Ensure you include them in your speeches and motto.

Another such device is the parallelism. A great example is Martin Luther King's 'I Have a Dream' speech, where he starts each sentence in an identical way. Parallelism is a rhetorical device in which parts of the sentence are grammatically the same, or a word, or a sequence of words is repeated. For example, the slogan from the British Tory electoral campaign was: ''New Labour, New Danger'' (which also rhymes by the way). And Putin won in 2018 with the straightforward slogan ''Strong President, Strong Russia.'' The sentence is divided into two parts, and both have the same structure *New + noun* or *Strong + noun*. In the same vein, the slogan of the victorious Jair Bolsonaro was ''Brasil acima de tudo, Deus acima de todos.'' (Brazil above everything, God above everyone.) It spells out his national conservative ideology through proper usage of this rhetorical trick. The sentence is subdivided into two parts, that have an identical grammatical structure and repeats the words *above every-*. Such parallelism is a great persuasive tool. It has symmetry, which allows listeners to memorize it more easily. And because the public, due to the repetitive structure, knows what to expect next, they digest the message more readily.

Which message to convey

Slogans can also tell something about yourself, for example, help you project an aura of honesty and authenticity. Abraham Lincoln had already gained a reputation of an upright lawyer and representative. He, with great care, manipulated his image so that he would appear as a straight-shooting, commonsense man of the people. So when running for president in 1860, his supporters and his electoral campaign ran with the motto ''Honest old Abe'' or the shorter ''Honest Abe''.

*

A fundamental psychological factor of human motivation is that we don't like failing. Therefore, several effective slogans talk about winning and success. This is somewhat a zero-sum view on the world: either you succeed or I do. Many slogans explicitly talk about victory or allude to it. One example is the slogan from Jacques Chirac, who later became President of France: ''Oui à la France qui gagne'' (Yes to a winning France) and ''Oui à la France qui invente'' (Yes to France, which invents). The human psyche has an aversion to losing. In the largest electoral success in modern Germany, Angela Merkel won the 2013 election with her party gaining 41.5% of the vote. She outstripped any opponent with her slogan ''Gemeinsam erfolgreich'' (Successful together).

The euphoria at soccer games and all kinds of other sports is interesting to observe. Whole crowds go ecstatic when the ball of their team crosses some line. The bandwagon effect is powerful once you get the ball rolling in your favor. The people will jump on the winning trend since victory is a profound desire of the human soul.

A case in point: after the disastrous and crushing defeat suffered in the Falklands War, the Argentinian Junta collapsed, and presidential elections were held. Playing onto those emotions, candidate Raul Alfonsin ran with the slogan ''Juntos para Argentina gane'' (together for an Argentinian win) and won the race. Talk about how you are going to win, your voters are going to succeed as well, and your country will flourish. They will love it.

*

A creative slogan is sometimes rewarding. Fidesz, the dominant party in Hungarian politics for decades, used to run with ''Don't vote for anyone over 35.'' That was when Viktor Orban, the leader of Fidesz, still was younger than 35; with age, he changed his slogan.

Another remarkable motto was from the French President Giscard d'Estaing. The Left generally prefers change, and the Right prefers that things remain how they are. Giscard d'Estaing was an unashamed centrist. He hence ran for office with ''Le Changement dans la Continuité'' (Change within Continuity), fusing the two sides. He won over centrist voters in the first round. In the second round, the French Right then rallied to his cause to block a victory of François Mitterrand, the candidate from the Left.

My country first

Another slogan, which the electorate never grows tired of, is ''[My Country] First!'' People namely prefer people that are similar to themselves. Those belonging to the same category (nationality, culture, race, language, etc.) will support each other more. This bias is ingrained in our genes dating back to the times we lived in small bands of hunter-gatherers. We thus have more affinity with related individuals; tribal affiliation is a universal law governing our behavior. There is even a Somali proverb which nails this down:

> ''Me against my brother.
>
> Me and my brother against the family.
>
> Me and my family against the clan.
>
> Me and my clan against my nation.
>
> Me and my nation against the world.''

The original ''America First'' was from the W.G. Harding—the victor of the 1920 US presidential election. With a mere two words, Warding succeeded in arousing and tapping into isolationist and anti-immigrant sentiments after the First World War. His message implies that his country and people will be favored. The attention and resources will be spent on your kin *first*, before others. And your nation will come *first* and win in the competition between nations.

Similarly, the Union Nationale won the general election in Québec in 1966 with ''Québec d'abord!'' (Québec first!) This message and its variations have, in the meantime, been reused so often that it has become cliché. Nevertheless, clichés became clichés in the first place because they work. Furthermore, the electorate doesn't have a good, reliable memory anyway, which is why slogans are so often reused.

''Let's Make America Great Again'' is a strong example from Ronald Reagan, twice President of the USA. It simultaneously projects a successful future, taps into the power of nostalgia, and blames the past administration for current woes. As a general rule, a slogan should trigger emotions in your public, and this message accomplishes this on multiple levels. It is about pathos, remember?

Donald Trump later reused the slogan, but dropped the ''let's''. Never create slogans longer than they need to be. And, as proven over and over again, in case you don't have a satisfying idea for a slogan, feel free to pick one from the past. That never stopped Donald Trump from winning, quite to the contrary. The practice of reusing slogans has become so common that it happens that two candidates accidentally select the same. For example, in the 2004 Austrian presidential campaign, the two largest parties (SPÖ and ÖVP) accused each other of stealing their slogan.

Be vague

What is great in the slogan ''Make America Great Again'' is that it is vague. ''Yes We Can'' as well can be interpreted in many ways. Yes We Can do what? This can be a wise strategy for a slogan, as it allows many people to decipher it in their own way. Each can then find him- or herself in it.

Furthermore, you won't let yourself being pinpointed by the press and your adversaries. Avoid being too precise; this will inevitably lead you to a defensive and reactive posture. Instead, by remaining intentionally vague, you can dodge enemy punches by claiming they misrepresent or misquote your statements. Cristina de Kirchner, who became President of Argentina, ran her campaign with ''Change is Just Beginning!'', yet another imprecise expression. On a side-note, she was later jailed for corruption.

Pick hence a slogan like ''Save our Children!'' Everyone loves kids and can get behind that message. At the same time, each voter will understand this message in a different way. ''Save Our Children''—of course!—But from whom? From Global Warming, Terrorists, Poverty, Mexicans, …

Appeal to the majority

A blatant appeal to the majority can work as well. Claim your opponents don't know the will of the people. Or worse even: they understand it, but due to their cynicism and arrogance, don't act on it. Joseph Estrada—originally an actor—won a landslide in the presidential campaign in the 1998 Philippine elections. His platform was based on helping the poor, who formed a majority in this third world country. ''Joseph Estrada for the Poor'' was his slogan. (As an anecdote, he was impeached three years later for outrageous amounts of corruption and was sentenced for plundering a casual $80m.)

The Brexit party in the United Kingdom ran with the basic and straightforward ''Brexit means Brexit.'' They thereby called upon the 52% that voted yes in the referendum on the exit of the

UK out of the EU. A more general illustration is the slogan ''For the Many, Not the Few,'' used by many contenders vying for the presidential position. It is so commonly used, that this has led to cases where both opposing sides wielded the equivalent or outright identical slogan. These are all in the vein of ''Power to the People'' or ''For the People''. Bill Clinton ran in 1992 with ''Putting People First.'' The popular internet meme ''We are the 99%'' is yet another illustration of this.

*

In Part I, you have seen how to build the right political program. Now condense it in a simple slogan to transmit your message to voters. The slogan should be short, easy to remember, and convey your core message while appealing to the electorate's emotions.

Part III -
Adapt to the political landscape

Chapter 9
Adjust to the voting mechanism

You have to learn the rules of the game.
And then you have to play better than anyone else.
— senator Dianne Feinstein

Your competitors' primary purpose is—like your own—the accumulation of political power. And for this purpose, you will apply ferociously the procedures described in this book. Yet to gain the vote of the public is not the only path to victory. Public opinion is not the only thing that matters. It is vital to pay attention to the institutional rules of the game and adapt your strategy accordingly.

Over the past chapters, I have gone over how you should set the content of your campaign, and how to transmit it. The strength of pathos—human emotions and subconscious behavior—was therein a determining factor.

But, in this part, let's take a step back and look at the machinery of democracy. How do democracies function and what are the rules governing elections? Is the president chosen in a one-turn vote or a two-turn vote? How can you exploit this to your advantage? In the USA, for illustration, it is not the one that wins the popular vote (most votes) that wins the presidency. Instead, the people elect the electoral college, which at its turn selects the president.

The rules to determine the winner influence your approach to the race. Moreover, the rules also affect voter intention in a predictable way, and you can take advantage of that.

In a naive view, democracy is an institutional arrangement where the people elect political decision-holders. Different individuals, most often grouped in political parties, try to obtain positions of power by swaying citizens to vote for them in periodic elections. Holding regular elections is, nevertheless, not sufficient to be a functioning democracy. Countries that don't hold elections such as the Kingdom of Saudi Arabia and the People's Republic of China are openly undemocratic. But there are other countries where elections are held that are only superficially democratic.

Essential for democracy is that individual rights are guaranteed and that the opposition stands a fair chance to win the next election. The current head of the executive could employ the administration and law enforcement agencies to silence, imprison, and condemn in unfair trials its political opponents. Or the government could ban any media company that displeases it. No fair, competitive elections are possible in those circumstances. More subtle is a subverted process whereby stringent rules apply to the presidential candidature. Those in power can disqualify other candidates and prevent them from presenting themselves. For example, contenders are made ineligible on the ground of not having gathered enough signatures or some other excuse. Such pseudo-democracies where the current men in power abuse of their might is all too common.

In 2015, Nursultan Nazarbayev won the election in Kazakstan with a comfortable 97.5% of the vote. This was better than in 2011, where he only scored 95.5% and 2005, where he only secured 91.15% and 1999 with 81%. The Kazakh capital was renamed from Astana to its present name Nur-Sultan in honor of his long rule. This illustrates how, in Kazakstan, the power does not lie with the voter, but with who counts the vote, as Stalin said. Such farcical, sham elections have also occurred to more or less degree in many countries, such as Iran, Venezuela, and to a lesser extent Turkey and Russia in the 21st century. In 2007, Venezuelan President Hugo Chávez banned Radio Caracas to dismantle the outlet of the opposition. And Erdogan, as Turkish President, blocked internet access to Reddit, Wikipedia, and Twitter. Our focus this chapter lies on mature and stable democracies, not on states backsliding towards authoritarianism.

The landscape of political parties

Let's first have a look at the legislative elections. There are multiple types of electoral systems for electing the legislature (also called Parliament, National Assembly, House of Representatives, etc.). This influences the structure of the political landscape and its fragmentation, and therefore impacts the presidential elections as well. The three most common methods are first-past-the-post, two-turn vote, and proportional.

In first-past-the-post (FPTP), the country is split into districts, each of which sends one representative to the legislation. The person who obtains the most votes in that district is elected, even if he or she didn't achieve an absolute majority (more than half of the valid votes cast). Such a system discourages small parties unless that party is geographically concentrated in a few of the country's districts.

Imagine an area where three political parties present a candidate. Party A and B are large, and score 48% respectively 45% of the vote. Party C is small and only scores 7%. In this case, party A would win the seat. Since party B is significant too, they could hope to win this seat back next election, as the margin of defeat was small. Party B likely won other districts, but party C seldom scores more than party A or B and, therefore, has few to no representatives. Large parties thrive when the legislature is elected with the FPTP voting mechanism. As a consequence, it leads to a system with few—often times two—significant political parties.

First-past-the-post is mostly practiced in Anglo-Saxon countries: United States, Great Britain, and its former colonies. The United States counts only two major parties, the Republicans and the Democrats. The Labor and the Conservative party dominate the United Kingdom. Two smaller parties in Great-Britain, such as the UKIP and the Lib-Dem, had trouble gaining seats. The Lib-Dems in the 1992 UK election won close to 18% of the vote, yet secured only 3% of the seats in Parliament. Same with the UKIP, which in the 2015 election won 12.6% of the vote, yet only got 1 out of 650 seats in Parliament.

Proportional systems, which are common in Continental Europe and South America, would, on the contrary, grant seats in the legislative house in a manner proportionate to the number of votes a party collected.

This method fractures the political landscape into many small parties. As each 5 to 10% party knows it can secure seats, there is no incentive to form 'big-tent' parties. Each party tends to be ideologically pure, instead of representing an array of interests and ideologies.

Two-turn systems are used in France, Iran, and former French colonies. It functions as follows: the country is divided into districts with one representative each. A first vote is held. One or two weeks thereafter, a second vote is held, with only the top two candidates from the first vote are on the ballot.

In practice, the incentives of the two-turn system lie somewhere in between FPTP and proportional. It favors large parties, but not as much the FPTP. The political landscape is less fractured as in proportional systems, but more than in FPTP.

Presidential election mechanism

Let's turn towards the presidential (s)election.

There are parliamentary systems where the president has few to no powers and is selected by the legislative (Italy, Germany, Israel) instead of directly elected by the people. Suffice to say that in such countries, if you want to become head of state, you have to be an old and experienced politician. The political class must respect you. The focus of this book does not lie on those systems.

Direct presidential elections worldwide can be divided into three systems: one-turn popular vote, two-turn election, and an electoral college voting mechanism. A one-turn vote (also called plurality vote) is enacted in countries like Mexico, Iceland, South-Korea, the Philippines, Paraguay, and Taiwan. Most other presidential countries introduced the two-turn system, first instituted in the French Fifth Republic (1958). The third way is through an indirect election where an electoral college selects the head of state: the people elect electors who, in turn, choose the president. This mechanism was more prevalent in the past (France, Finland, Bolivia, Paraguay, and others used it) and is still in use in the USA. The US case has special incentives and deserves a separate analysis. There are other mechanisms as well, such as single transferable vote to elect the President of Ireland. Still, they are rare and I won't dwell on them.

Your strategy should depend on the political landscape and the presidential election mechanism.

(A) Plurality vote with only two major parties

Countries with the first-past-the-post method of selecting the legislature and a one-turn ballot for the presidency naturally produce a two-party system. The USA, divided into the Republican and Democratic Party, is a classic example. Another example is Nigeria (All Progressives Congress vs. People's Democratic Party). Each party occupies roughly half of the political space and has a decent shot at ruling. In such a case, you have to **become the nominee of one of the two major parties**. Capturing a party will be discussed in the next chapter.

In such a bipolar political landscape, it is a rare exception to see more than two candidates with a shot at winning. In the 1992 presidential election, for the first time in a long while, there were three serious contenders in the USA. Next to the usual Democratic and Republican, a third, independent candidate arose. The iconoclastic Ross Perot attempted to seize the White House and eventually scored close to 19% of the vote. Styling himself a result-oriented outsider to Washington, he had a good shot at winning the three-person race. His unique background and unconventional style caught attention. His campaign content was strong, applying many strategies described before. His economic program blamed Mexico (in particular the free trade deal NAFTA) and pointed at the looming national debt. His political manifesto was rich with well-liked promises and proposals so that his popularity was high among both Democrats and Republicans. Yet he squandered it all by his paranoia and distrust of his team. His behavior was erratic (leaving the race, later reentering it). He further questioned the loyalty of his staff and refused to follow their advice. All this was foolish and caused a drop in polls.

But even if Perot had run the perfect campaign, it was unlikely he would have defeated both major parties. 19% is a decent result in these political circumstances and a testimony to his popularity. It would have been a respectable score in a parliamentary democracy. Conversely, in a presidential country, there is only one winner. Don't aim at being second or third, for this is a total waste. That is why it is not advised to run as an independent in these circumstances because it is too difficult.

(B) Plurality vote with multiple candidates

With more than two candidates, anything could happen. In a plurality vote, there can be only one winner in the one and only election. Often, a candidate will win with less than 50% of the ballots in favor of his or her candidacy.

Let's examine the historical case of the 1970 Chilean election to understand what could occur. There were three major candidates, each approximately polling at 1/3 of the vote.

Allende won with a bit more than a third of the vote. Both losers thought they could win and, therefore, didn't back down. After the election, they regretted this and realized they should have formed an alliance instead of spoiling each other.

1970 Chilean election results

Candidate	Ideology	Result
Salvador Allende	left-wing (socialist)	36.61%
Jorge A. Rodríguez	right-wing (conservative)	35.27%
Radomiro Tomi	centre (christian-democrat)	28.11%

A somewhat similar event occurred in the 1987 Korean presidential election. The Reunification Democratic Party in the opposition was polling well and was destined to win. But then the party split in two: Kim Young-sam (28% of vote) retained control of the party, but Kim Dae-jung (27% of vote) founded a new one. They ran separately and so allowed the third candidate Roh Tae-woo to win. The winner only gathered 36.6% of the vote, much less than both opposition candidates combined (55%).

If you find yourself in a likewise situation, you have to **avoid being spoiled**. Take example on the 2002 South-Korean election. Three major candidates emerged during the campaign: Roh, Chung, and Lee. It seemed clear that if both Roh and Chung ran, Lee would win. Instead of running separately and competing against each other, Roh and Chung decided to combine their strength. They so avoided splitting the vote, as had occurred in the 1987 South-Korean election. The problem that here arises is, who steps down and who remain? It is a bit of an ego bluffing game. Eventually, Roh and Chung agreed on conducting polls where the winner would run as the unified candidate. Roh won and Chung stepped down. Both candidates so join forces and made a power-sharing agreement.

Roh would win the presidential election thanks to this. He later ended up on bad terms with Chung, who felt betrayed because he was not involved enough in policy decisions. Whether you keep up your formal assurance to share power after your victory is up to you.

(C) Plurality vote with many parties

If there are many parties, you will have to build coalitions to succeed. This is a typical case when legislative elections are held with a proportional or a two-turn system. A small, 5% party in a proportional election can expect to win 5% of the seats. In contrast, when it comes to the presidential election, it will lose. The party and its voters have to ally themselves with their second (or third) preferred choice. Moreover, large parties often win or lose presidential elections with small margins ($<1\%$). The large parties thus have incentives to seek alliances with small groups to tilt them first over the finish line. If you are the nominee such a large party, you cannot afford to turn away potential allies in a close race.

In Mexico, part of the Chamber of Deputies is elected part by FPTP and part proportionally. There are, as of 2018, nine political parties that sit in the Chamber. In the 2018 presidential election, three major candidates (Andrés Manuel López Obrador, Ricardo Anaya, José Antonio Meade) were each supported by coalitions of three parties. For illustration, Ricardo Anaya was supported by the center-right PAN, the leftist PRD, and the Citizens' Movement as well. The Citizens' Movement had, however, in the 2012 election supported the other candidate (López Obrador) instead. So every election can give rise to new coalitions.

The Chilean presidential election also features coalitions of parties. It is not rare to see more than half a dozen parties bundle forces. As a candidate of one party, you must ally yourself with other parties in that case. Form what is called a 'big tent' coalition. In a big-tent, you will have to aggregate multiple interests, political ideologies, and social classes.

Another wise move is to take a vice-president that complements you. In a fractured political landscape such as Brazil, take a vice-president (VP) from another party to cement your alliance and broaden your base. In the USA, take as VP someone from your party that holds different views to your own, or is from another geographical area, or the other gender, or another race.

Taiwanese politics are more bipolar than Mexican because most of the parliament is elected through FPTP. The two largest parties are the KMT (center-right) and DPP (center-left). Other parties never hold more than 8% combined of the seats of the legislature, often less, even though they have a much higher vote share. For the presidential elections, the two largest parties seek to ally themselves with the smaller parties. Even a tiny extra vote share can win or lose the election. In practice, the presidential election is always decided between the so-called ''Pan-Blue'' coalition (led by the KMT) and the ''Pan-Green'' coalition (led by the DPP).

It is even okay to ally extreme elements as long as you are not personally tainted. You namely have to build a broad coalition to win a plurality. Hence cast a wide ideological net to secure the most votes. You should remain perceived as a moderate, though, so that you don't scare away other allies.

In summary, you need **to assemble a broad interparty coalition**. Promise that once you are president, you will allocate cabinet seats to your allies to reward them for their support. Include some of their pet policies into your program. You can so attract endorsements and support from other parties.

(D) Two-turn vote

Most presidencies nowadays adopted the two-turn popular vote as a mechanic for selecting the president. This originates in the French Fifth Republic. In the first round, a candidate wins if he or she has more than 50% of the valid votes. If no candidates achieve a majority of the votes—which usually happens—, there is a runoff election between the two candidates with most votes in the first round. This method has been adopted by most presidential and semi-presidential countries, such as France, Brazil, Finland, Austria, Romania, Portugal, most of Central and South-America, and Africa.

In the first turn, people will vote for their favorite candidate (also called the heart's choice). Often in the second vote, the center-left and center-right candidate will be left standing. People will then vote for the least bad candidate remaining or abstain from voting. Choosing the lesser evil in the second vote is also called the reasoned choice.

In a one turn popular vote, political players forge alliances before elections. In a two-round system, however, small candidates of each party will try their best in the first round. After the first round, they will call upon their voters to vote for one of the two remaining candidates. Generally, they pick those that are ideologically the closest.

In the 2002 French race, sixteen candidates ran in the first round. The vote was very dispersed. The French left was so split that the center-left Lionel Jospin from the Socialist party shockingly didn't make it to the second round. He ended up third behind the extreme-right Front-National candidate Jean-Marie Le Pen. In the runoff, the center-right candidate J. Chirac won a crushing victory as the whole electorate voted for him to ward off the extreme-right candidate. A spoiler effect can thus also occur in two-turn systems.

In the Iranian 2005 election, the reformists, if united, would have made the second round. However, multiple reformist candidates split the vote. That allowed, against all expectation, Ahmadinejad to pass to the second round and later win.

In the 2017 French election, something similar happened. The major center-left party popularity collapsed. Left-inclined citizens spread their vote over the extreme-left, the classical left, and the new centrist party. In the middle of the campaign, a scandal came to light, hitting the center-right candidate. The newly formed centrist political party En Marche, led by Emmanuel Macron, profited from this by sucking up voters from the center-left and center-right. In the first round, he gained the most votes together with the extreme right Marine Le Pen. In the runoff, Macron smashed Le Pen by virtue of being a centrist in the middle of the political landscape.

The recurring French left-wing infighting has been pathetic and completely stupid. In a two-turn system, you have to pass the first round foremost. In 2002, all pollsters were expecting the socialist candidate to win—not only the first round but the second round as well. Yet the socialist candidate ended up losing it all. The disunity was not only confined to politicians vying for power, but also its electorate didn't care. Voting is a statement. Sometimes it seems the people don't even want to win; they only want to express themselves at the polling booth. Voting for a chance-less candidate makes many happy. And so spoiling keeps occurring.

So, how to win in a two-turn system? First, win the first turn. Then win the second. For winning the first turn, it is essential **to target a large base**. A favorable case would be to win the primary of the large center-left or center-left party, which you can find in near-all countries. Next, ally parties that have overlapping policy proposals and a similar ideology, and would otherwise drain voters from you. Avoid at all cost too many ideologically close opponents as happened to the French left in 2002 and 2017, or the Iranian reformists in 2005. Such a split vote is to the benefit of your adversaries at the other end of the political landscape.

For example, the eventual winner of the French 2017 election, Emmanuel Macron, executed a smart move by allying with François Bayrou. In exchange, Macron would support Bayrou's proposals and grant his party ministerial posts. Bayrou's views resembled those of Macron, and there were no hurdles or vetoes between them. Bayrou was a significant player (gaining 18 % in 2007 and 9% in 2012), and allying him was a judicious move. Their coalition increased the odds of reaching the second turn. Without it, both would have faltered in the first round. You, too, should seek alliances with players within close political distance.

Develop your program to ensure you don't end up being a one-trick pony candidate. You have to please a broad set of the electorate to grab at least the second place. Single issue candidates and parties like the greens, the anti-immigration party, the pirate party, or those that represent a small ethnic or religious group, rarely achieve 15%, let stand 50% of the vote. In a parliamentary system, you might be content with that score and even maneuver yourself in the government. Yet in presidential runs, you would always fail if you run on a single issue. Capture an already large party, or forge alliances amid small, and cast a wide net instead. That, together with what was set forth in previous chapters, will guarantee a top-two finish in the first turn. Your name on the ballot of the second turn is so secured.

In a one-turn election with two candidates, you have to be a centrist already in the first and sole turn. In a two-turn system, **gravitate towards the center of the political spectrum in the second turn** if you haven't already before.

Often, there are only two candidates who have a shot at winning the presidency. This happens by design in the second round of a two-turn presidential election. But it is a natural phenomenon of the one-round vote as well. It will then be advantageous for you to gravitate towards the center. Some voters are left-wing, others right-wing, and others centrist. Each country has a median voter, who holds the average political views. By taking more moderate stances, you will win your wing and the centrists, while your opponent will only obtain the vote of one wing. This is because the centrist will favor the candidate that is politically the closest to them. Thus almost all presidential election mechanisms favor candidates that align the most with the median voter.

Some have declared that it is judicious to produce a bold left- or right-wing policy program to encourage voter turnout in your base. They assert that taking a centrist position generates less excitement and results in a lower base turnout. These political pundits claim it is about riling up your base. "Pretend to go to war against the other,'' they say. But this is the wrong advice. You should instead temper your tone to persuade precious swing, moderate voters. With extreme viewpoints, you drive away moderates/centrists and also increase voter turnout on the other side. You don't want to motivate the other team to show up.

For example, Barry Goldwater didn't follow this advice at all. In consequence, he suffered a massive defeat. Goldwater was the presidential candidate of the Republican Party in the 1964 US election. He was considered quite extreme, because he wanted to confront the Soviets and cut social security. Since the voters at the primary are different from those voting at the general election, it could make sense to hold extremer views at first. For a primary ballot, pander to the primary voters. These are often different than those in the general election. Thereafter, one should tone down. Yet Goldwater rejected any centrist pivot, even after he won the primary. He hence alienated many more moderate Republicans and independent centrists. Goldwater lost, scoring only 38% of the popular vote to Johnson's 61%. It was the largest margin in 200 years of US history. Goldwater kept being branded as an extremist and a warmonger, yet refused to cede any of his positions. While he gained a reputation for steadfastness, this is not sufficient to win. A bit of flexibility in one's ideology is required.

Through persuasion, you can rarely shift voters in your direction. It is wiser you gravitate towards the center of mass. Abandoning your morals and ideology is preferable over abandoning victory.

The US Democratic Party committed that same mistake eight years later. McGovern was appointed as the Democratic candidate after a hotly contested primary. McGovern ran on a platform of immediately ending the Vietnam War and promising guaranteed minimum incomes for the poor. The electorate perceived this as too radical. McGovern, for this reason, lost to Nixon by a large margin.

Lula da Silva had stubbornly been second place in many Brazilian presidential elections. Lula had, in the past, openly defended a transition to a socialist economy. Feared for his extreme left-wing views, investors' confidence in the country would drop when Lula gained in the polls. In past campaigns, other contestants picked him apart with this (they called it the ''Lula risk''). In the 2002 campaign, Lula changed his mind and wrote his 'Letter to the Brazilian People'. Therein, he promised that if he won the election, he would not change the economic policy of Brazil. Some on the Left saw this shift to the center from Lula with a critical eye. Yet for once, the moderate voters favored him over his opponent. In this fashion, Lula da Silva and the Brazilian Left won after decades of losses.

Alexander van der Bellen from the left-wing Green Austrian party managed to pass the first round of the two-turn vote in 2016. For the second round, he appealed to the political center. With his slogan ''Unser Präsident der Mitte'' (Our President of the Center), he won over centrists to his side. This winning maneuver is prevalent in most presidential elections.

As already discussed, two political parties (DPP and KMT) dominate Taiwanese politics. The island of Taiwan (officially named the Republic of China) has strained relations with China (officially called the People's Republic of China). Historically, Taiwan used to be part of China. Because of a civil war, Taiwan is now de facto independent. The Taiwanese political spectrum is defined in terms of Taiwanese independence (supported by the

DPP) versus an eventual Chinese reunification (supported by the KMT). However, when campaigning, astute candidates take moderate positions on this issue. The reason for this is that people who back either independence or unification have already decided for whom they will vote. For example, staunch proponents of independence will never vote KMT anyway. The goal of the campaign is, therefore, to capture the moderate middle.

Further examples abound. Before the 2016 US presidential election, the electorate considered Donald Trump to be more centrist than Hillary Clinton. Compared to other GOP primary candidates, Trump was not opposing Obamacare as much, less vocal on the public deficit, and had no stand on Abortion or LGBTQ. Trump's only extreme viewpoint was on immigration. That is, however, a good strategy, as mentioned in a previous chapter. Trump furthermore opposed the Iraq War. He vowed to avoid new Middle Eastern military adventures. Consequently, he won over the independents (who are not affiliated with either party) and defeated his opponent.

(E) Electoral College

Let's at last look at the electoral college mechanism in the United States. In the USA, each of the fifty states and the district of Washington obtain a number of electors. This number depends on the population of the state but slightly overweighs small states. The electors then elect the president by a majority of their vote cast. While it resembles the one-turn popular vote, some of the election rules influence the race. The important difference to (A) is the 'winner-takes-all' principle. As a candidate, it suffices to win a majority of the popular vote in a state to win all its electors.

It doesn't matter if you have a 50.01% or 100% result within a state; both lead to the capture of all its electors.

So what should you do? First, start with the realization that winning a state with a narrow margin versus winning it with a large one doesn't impact the result. A large margin causes wasted votes. On the flip side, losing a state by a slim margin is disastrous. Your opponent would capture all electors of that state. And all votes for you in that state are, in that case, de facto worthless. You should hence avoid concentrating in 2-3 populous states. Instead, distribute your support in a spatially even way. The optimal victory would be to win each state with a 0.01% lead. That would cause you to seize the entire electoral college.

In practice, **concentrate on winning battleground states**. These are states where the race between you and your opponent is the closest. It is even worthwhile to relocate your residence there, to gain a small edge over your adversaries. There is no point in focusing on states where you are far ahead. Idem with states where you are far behind. You will anyway pick up all their electors, or respectively none of them. Any campaigning in those places will be fruitless.

The presidential election in the USA does not guarantee that the one with the most votes wins. In five close United States elections (1824, 1876, 1888, 2000, and 2016), the candidate who won the popular vote still lost the election. It is foolish to think in terms of popular vote in such a system. Who wins that vote is irrelevant.

There are always those amateurs that complain in chess after they suffer a loss. They come up with statements that they ''captured more pieces than their opponent.'' But that is not how it works. Chess is won by checkmating, not by capturing pieces.

Professionals focus on checkmating. They without remorse sacrifice pieces for a better shot at victory.

Your attention should be on the rules to capture power. Gaining vote share often helps—just like capturing pieces in chess—but not always.

Provisions favoring small states in federal or confederate nations are not unusual. Same with those requiring a certain geographical spread. Other political entities than the USA—like Belgium, Switzerland, or the European Union—also favor smaller states. In Indonesia, the winner needs to win a minimum of 20% in more than half of the provinces.

Federations institute such rules to prevent that a single populous state dominates the presidential election. Candidates are forced to seek some support across regions and spread out geographically. The Belgian constitution grants half of the ministerial posts to the French-speaking minority, which compose 40% of the population. Similar provisions exist in other countries, such as Lebanon.

Regarding the electoral college, it is worth examining the skillful 2016 campaign of Donald J. Trump. Despite losing the popular vote, he comfortably won the electoral vote. This mastermind grasped the implications of the presidential selection mechanism.

Evolution in the most populous states

State	Republican margin 2012	Republican margin 2016	Evolution
California	-23.1%	-30.1%	-7.0%
Texas	+15.8%	+9.0%	-6.8%

When comparing his results to the Republican nominees in previous elections, observe that he lost voters in states where the Republicans were heavily favored (-6.8% in Texas, for example). Yet he maintained sufficient support to win them. Also, notice how he lost in Democratic-leaning states (7% margin decrease compared to 2012 in California). But those votes don't matter since losing a state by 0.1% is the same as losing it with 30%.

Evolution in battleground states

State	Republican margin 2012	Republican margin 2016	Evolution
Florida	-0.9%	+1.2%	+2.1%
Wisconsin	-7.0%	+0.8%	+7.8%
Pennsylvania	-5.4%	+0.7%	+6.1%
Michigan	-9.5%	+0.2%	+9.7%

The winner-takes-all logic from state to state delivers the deciding vote to the few so-called swing states. Trump won those. He eked out a win in Florida (1.2%), Wisconsin (0.8%), Pennsylvania (0.7%), and Michigan (0.2%). By contrast, the inept Hillary Clinton only won one state with a margin of less than 1.5% (New Hampshire, a small state). She increased her popular vote in two most populous states (California, Texas) to no avail. Raking your score in a state you were already going to win or lose does not alter the outcome.

Now the pieces fall into place. Why did Trump pick the Mexicans as his go-to-blame minority? It is simple realpolitik. It lost him votes elsewhere, but it won him over the battleground states. Those parts of America are predominantly white, more so than average, and contain few Hispanic voters that felt alienated by Trump's rhetoric. Why did Trump vowed to act against China? The pivotal regions in the election have suffered from relative economic decline owing to the deindustrialization (the so-called Rust Belt region). In almost every public speech, Trump discussed protectionism against China. He sponsored policies to serve that particular group of people who had suffered from globalization. Trump's proposed tariffs on China did not fall in deaf ears. It played a crucial role in winning Michigan, Wisconsin, and Pennsylvania.

That was the right strategy to take control of the White House. Donald Trump factored in the rules of the game and played better than Hillary Clinton. And so Trump clutched the presidency. Like him, you should tilt the odds in your favor by taking advantage of the rules of the game.

*

At this point, some of you might claim that a good set of presidential election rules would render such strategizing and craftiness impossible. Only, it is difficult to have the perfect method for choosing the president. It was even outright proven to be mathematically impossible unless there is exactly one voter deciding. The mathematician Kenneth Arrow demonstrated this in 1951, and won the Nobel Prize for his contributions. This means there is always room for outdoing your opponent in this realm. So study the electoral mechanisms to your advantage.

*

My advice is to respect the rules of the game in a modern democracy and not try cheating them. I do not write this as a moral imperative but as a practical warning. Reason is that democracy enjoys a favorable view amid the population. Any revelation of manipulation or circumvention of the electoral laws will be wielded against you. In the 21st century, the digital age, social media allows for rapid diffusion of allegations of electoral fraud and associated discontent. Breaking the rules (even if these are tacit rules) can backfire and discredit your candidacy for life.

In the 2014 Romanian presidential election, Victor Ponta was a favorite to obtain the highest mandate. Nonetheless, he did not heed these words of caution. Romania was still a young, unsophisticated, and less deeply institutionalized democracy. Electoral abuses existed and till then were tolerated. An influencing factor in the 2014 election were the voters from the large Romanian diaspora. Ponta wasn't polling well with this part of the electorate. Foreign Minister Titus Corlatean of the same party, rendered voting abroad on purpose difficult to favor Ponta's candidacy. This led to riots amid the Romanians outside the country. They had to wait for hours at the polling booth. Many were unable to express their vote in the first round of the presidential election (voting stops at 9 p.m.).

It caused a massive backslash against Ponta. The exasperated Romanians living overseas organized themselves through social media (the diaspora is younger and more educated than those at home). They turned up in huge numbers in the second round, waited patiently till they could vote, and piled up against Ponta, who only obtained 10% of the vote abroad. On record turnout, Ponta, who had scored more than 40% in the first round, was defeated. In a total surprise and coming from a ten percentage point deficit in the first round, Klaus Iohannis snatched the office of president. The turnout was 53.17% in the first round and a record 64.10% in the second round. Generally, the count of voters in the second round is lower since all but two candidates have dropped out. A higher turnout in the second round is uncommon, and Ponta's egregious manipulation attempts caused it. His arrogance and underestimation of the growing strength of democratic rule caused the upset and so lost him the election.

*

Dear reader, I cannot foresee how the circumstances will be in your country in the future. The examples given within this chapter are from past or contemporary times. It is up to you to apply the transmitted knowledge. Adapt your strategy and the concepts learned in previous chapters to the rules of the game and the situation at hand. And never forget: it is winning that matters. The rest is secondary.

Chapter 10
Capture or found a party

There is no act of treachery or meanness
of which a political party is not capable;
for in politics there is no honor
— Benjamin Disraeli

What is the function of political parties in your victory? A party is a candidate selection group. It is a machine that spits out candidates for the office of president. Capturing or founding a political party is an essential step in the electoral process. It will give you a stage from which you will address to the nation and hence greatly help you disseminating your program.

Once you become their candidate, you will be able to count on the party's support. This happens because your party, like any other political party, strives for political supremacy for itself. A political party has a degree of tribalism; it glues the people together. Parties have a loyal base that will support and vote for the party's candidate no matter what. They will, furthermore, assist you since having a president in office is usually a huge advantage to the party. It gives the party a mouthpiece and an advocate at the highest level. Moreover, the president has the exclusive right to constitute the executive branch. If you win, you will distribute offices and positions of power in the government to reward the loyalty of the party members. Also, the legislative election is correlated with the presidential election. A popular candidate for the presidency can carry his or her party. For illustration, the Brazilian PSL was a small party, but thanks to the popular Jair Bolsanaro, who won the presidential race, the PSL became second largest in the Chamber of Deputies.

There are four ways to become a candidate with a shot at winning:

(A) Be selected by a party

This way is the classical approach and many candidates took this path. Most historical cases belong to this category. The party elite decide who the candidate is. You will encounter opposition within the party; you will need to win the internal struggle against the many power-hungry rivals. The odds are in favor of longtime loyal insiders who have gained prominence within the party. The ideal case is if you have already served in the executive (minister, state governor) so that you can claim experience.

(B) Overtake a party

It is very doable to capture a party when there are open primaries. Originally from the United States, open primaries are a growing trend across the world. To win an open-primary, you will need name-recognition. Cultivate a loyal core of supporters with high turnout in the primary ballot. This is important because participation in primaries is meager compared to the actual election. Even if your base doesn't constitute a majority, you can win by firing them up and get them to the polls.

The advantage of overtaking a party is that you capture intact a whole party, its base, its public relation machinery, etcetera. Recent trends in the candidate selection mechanism foster this method; it is your easiest way to become a candidate with a shot at winning.

Examples of this are Donald J. Trump in the 2016 US election, who had only recently acquired membership to the Republican Party and was a member of the Democratic Party before. He was an outsider to the mainstream Republican Party elite. A lot of prominent Republicans opposed him, but once Trump had won, they closed ranks and stood behind him.

Jair Bolsanaro, in the 2018 Brazilian election, followed a similar path. In early 2018, Bolsanaro became a member of the Social-Liberal Party (PSL). This happened less than a year before the election. The previous leaders were ousted as Bolsanaro seized control and usurped the party. PSL occupied a centrist spot in the political landscape when Bolsanaro joined, but he steered it to the right and won the race.

This entire book can be employed to win a primary as well as a general election. In a primary, though, adapt all advice from this text to the electorate of the primary ballot.

(C) Create your own party

This is difficult as it requires you to create everything from scratch, attract members, and organize them. It is only possible if you are already well-known or can profit from the collapse of another party which causes an exodus to your party. The advantage, though, is that you are guaranteed to be the party's candidate because you will at first maintain control as its founder.

There are precedents for this. Emmanuel Macron, who was the minister of economy, quit his post before the next French presidential election. He abandoned the sinking ship that was the French Socialist Party. Next, he founded his party, La République En Marche. He saw an opportunity in the collapsing center-left socialist party and jumped on it. He then cemented his alliance with Bayrou, another major centrist candidate, and formed a credible centrist block. Fortunately for Macron, scandals then hit the center-right. His centrist party so swelled by the collapse of the major center-right and center-left parties.

Another case is from the Italian media tycoon Silvio Berlusconi. He founded his party, Forza Italia, in 1994. The two major Italian parties, the social democrats and the christian democrats, were collapsing under a multitude of corruption scandals. This created a vacuum in the political landscape which Berlusconi exploited. In the next 20 years, he dominated Italian politics and became multiple times prime minister.

(D) Run as an independent

Some independent candidates with a shot at winning were previously within a large party. They only run as an independent to pretend they are above politics and closer to the people. This is smart, although it requires that you already have significant name-recognition.

The most common cases of successful independent candidates are comedians and actors wanting to become head of state. In 2019, the comedian Zelensky came to power in Ukraine, obtaining close to three-quarters of the vote. Beppe Grillo, another comedian, founded the 5-Star Movement in Italy. The party, after a couple of electoral successes, eventually acquired the post of prime minister. Both Ronald Reagan and Arnold Schwarzenegger were famous actors before being elected Governor of California. Ronald Reagan, after that, became two-times President of the United States. The US Constitution requires any candidate to be a born Citizen. Schwarzenegger is hence not allowed to run for the presidency as he was born with Austrian nationality. There have though already been calls to amend the constitution to enable Schwarzenegger to participate in the race. Coluche, the most famous French comedian, also tried to run in 1981. Although he was polling well, he ultimately abandoned and retracted his candidacy. These individuals can profit from their celebrity status and are untainted by the political bickering in the capital. They can play well on ethos.

Your approach

Which is the best way? First, assess the political circumstances in your country.

In proportional systems with many political parties, each party tends to be ideologically pure. That is, each party caters to a specific subset of voters (class, ethnicity, religion, ideology, geography). Such parties will select insiders who are longtime loyal servants of the party. Therefore, method (A) is preferred, especially when the parties remain stable and gather a similar amount of votes in each election.

In countries with few political parties, the dynamic is different, and outsiders stand a good chance. Donald J. Trump, for example, was an outsider to the Republican Party when he ran in their primary. That would not be possible when the party kept a tight control of the selection system. But when there are only two 'big tent' parties, these are tempted to adopt selection systems such as open-primaries. These are on purpose accessible to outsiders. This is necessary because a major party in a first-past-the-post country needs to cultivate a broad base. Method (B), capturing an existing party, is favored in those circumstances.

If there are many medium-sized parties such as in Mexico, Brazil, and most European countries, but there have been significant shifts in the political landscape, then method (C) is preferred. If voters are not loyal to parties, or if scandals hit a major party, it is feasible to found a new party and acquire double-digit polls. These were the conditions for both Emmanuel Macron's and Silvio Berlusconi's successes. You will then need to maneuver and forge alliances with other parties.

Some countries have parties with an extremely loyal base, such in the USA. Studies have observed increasing polarization and distrust of the other party. (This was notably studied by asking parents if they would accept their child marrying someone from the other party.) There is evidence that US voters don't see the vote as much on ideological terms anymore. Many Americans support a party because they identify with it and oppose the other party, regardless of ideology. It becomes a game of us versus them. In that case, method (C) and (D) are close to impossible; you have to run as a candidate of a major and established party. Winning the primary of one of the two major parties is then basically necessary to win the presidential election.

Method (D), running as an independent, works best when there is a lot of disillusionment and distrust towards the political class. It bears no surprise that this approach was successful in countries like Ukraine and Italy, where the trust of the government and the institutions runs low.

Pounce at the right moment

When should you make a bid for power? Be opportunistic on the timing. The key to victory is not only building a strong candidacy but also waiting until the opposition is weak. This will maximize your odds of winning. You don't want to blow your chance against strong contenders. There will always be a next election.

Bide your time and then dash forward with all your might when the opportunity arises. Wait for an economic recession, a military defeat, or a scandal weakens the incumbent or your rivals.

Jair Bolsanaro's case provides us a valuable example. The center-left Workers' Party had delivered the previous president, Dilma Rousseff. But in 2016, Mrs. Rousseff got impeached in a corruption scandal. At the same time, Lula da Silva, another former president from the Workers' Party, was jailed for another corruption case. That made his party historically disliked, since its two most prominent politicians were now in jail. Fernando Haddad, a former associate of Lula da Silva, was next selected as the new candidate of the Workers' Party. Bolsanaro then launched his bid for president vowing to block the return of the unpopular but still large Workers' Party. And so he defeated Haddad, whose party was haunted by the past scandals.

*

In summary, by affiliating yourself with a party, you gain credibility on the national stage. You also benefit from the party's machinery and the loyalty of its members. It is an essential step required for broadcasting your message. The party will serve as a platform from which you can spread your political manifesto you have drafted in Part I of this book. Your approach should depend on the political landscape, to maximize your chances of victory.

Part IV -
Who you are

Chapter 11
Be a leader

A leader is a dealer in hope
— Napoleon Bonaparte

If you follow the guidance of previous chapters, you should already have caused excitement. Your program should generate a lot of emotions (pathos) in the right places. But a third or more of your success will be based on your personality.

The advent of social media reinforces and promotes this tendency, since it allows you to address your followers directly. In the past, voters couldn't follow one candidate as closely as today. They instead relied more on intermediaries, such as local representatives of the party and the reporting in traditional media. The development of internet made it easier for one personality to dominate the scene, instead of relying on party structures and press organization as in the past. You can nowadays hence avoid or bash traditional media.

Your virtues

Your character and ability matter. A third of the people admit voting based on some aspect of a candidates' personal characteristic (ethos). Many more do so subconsciously. This chapter analyses this impact and sets forth recommendations. What should your character be like?

Studies and polls have demonstrated that three traits are admired and deemed necessary. All three are essential in convincing the public to vote for you. These are trustworthiness, leadership, and competence. You have to project at all times an aura of all three to be successful. Through your actions and words, you will demonstrate that you have those qualities and so convince voters to vote for you. If you lack those virtues, rivals will be able to discredit your candidacy. Never let an opponent's attack go unanswered if it accuses you of an absence of those virtues. You have to prove every day (1) that you are an honest, trustworthy person, with a lot of personal integrity; (2) that you are a leader, someone they can follow; (3) that you are experienced, bright, and will manage the administration with skill.

(1) Honesty

The fact that the electorate gives so much weight to integrity is understandable. When a candidate makes so many promises (and you will need to), the people wish that he or she also keeps them.

Once someone is elected president, that person gains considerable power. A president cannot be ousted except for outright impeachment. Impeachment is a long and tedious procedure that requires super-majorities in all countries and hence rarely occurs. Breaking a promise is not an impeachable deed, so nothing holds a winner back to renege on past promises. When voters vote for you, they lay their destiny in your hands for a couple of years. They have no way of revoking your mandate. Contrary to parliamentary systems, no early elections are possible. Neither can parliament cause your fall and exclude you from the executive with a simple motion of no-confidence. So once elected, the voters are at the mercy of the president, who can with impunity break any campaign pledges. This leads the public to a natural distrust of any of your statements and promises given.

You pretend to defend the people, pledge to implement their favorite, pet policies, and vow to serve the good of the nation to the best of your abilities. But will people believe you? Talk is cheap after all. Even if you promise what they like, this can be diminished if they perceive you as untrustworthy. Before entrusting you with so much power, people will judge you on your integrity.

How do you gain their confidence? You should highlight past achievements and kept promises. Even better is to have others vouch for you. People give a lot of weight to endorsements of well-known or authoritative persons. Have your significant other or a previous well-liked president vouch for your integrity. That is much more effective than any rational argument you could conjure.

When you communicate, don't say fuzzy or complex phrases. Keep to simple and straightforward statements. Tell it like it is rather than sugarcoating issues in your country. Being frank and direct can pay off. This builds up your reputation as an honest person. Of course, don't lie, unless the truth would hurt your campaign even more. Don't change your program too often within one campaign cycle, although you have to change in between cycles. You namely need to adapt to the mood of the country: retain your popular proposals and oppose those that became unpopular. Pay furthermore attention to your body language. People will look for clues of your (lack of) integrity.

Look at the history of reputable presidents. Abraham Lincoln earned his nickname, ''Honest Abe'', before the presidential election. His character was the determining factor in winning his party's nomination.

And before participating in the 1946 Argentinian presidential election, Juan Perón built up his reputation. In the years before, he led the Labor Department, back then a small state agency of little political importance. He sided with the unions and acted against large ranchers, keeping all promises he made. After the 1944 San Juan earthquake, Perón took charge of the fundraising effort for the relief efforts. It earned him widespread public recognition and approval. His marriage with the popular and beloved Eva Perón boosted the public's appreciation of his character.

He would go on to win three presidential elections. Juan Perón remains the most iconic Argentinian President. His success was caused not only by his well-strategized platform but also by his cleverly engineered reputation of an honest and caring man. His persona spawned the Peronist movement that thrives till today.

On the flip side, undermine the perception of your opponents' honesty at every occasion. Denounce other contestants when they change their minds; call such unreliable persons flip-floppers. Never hesitate to highlight yet another broken promise of your opponents and point at their sinister motives. Through ads, speeches, and debates, sow doubt about their real intent.

Dig into their past to find that one little mistake they once made and exploit it. One careless remark they made can be used to make them appear insincere and so assassinate their character. Carry out a deliberate and sustained effort to damage their reputation and credibility. Don't let adversaries gain the upper hand in this domain. As recommended in a previous chapter, you should spend enough on opposition research to find your adversary's flaws and past cover-ups.

(2) Leadership

Humans are at their core social animals, which is why we intuitively value leadership. We have in-built mechanisms that regulate our behavior and stratify human groups. We are genetically conditioned to expect hierarchies and to respect authority. People long for someone who takes initiative and responsibility. The masses crave for a leader, who is expected to be calm, confident, and dominant. It is your role to fulfill people's expectations of a leader.

You keep your cool even in tense situations. Often the press, your opponent, or a passing pedestrian will criticize, interrupt, or challenge you with a difficult question. Don't let them catch you off guard. Rather retort with a witty one-liner in a light-hearted manner.

A further mistake is hedging your political discourse by employing words such as 'sort of', 'somewhat', 'to some extent', or 'partially'. Humans have doubts and hesitations. They expect the president to have none because this soothes them (similar to children who are reassured by their parents). That is why you should talk with confidence and authority and forgo hedging statements. You will so generate more controversy, which is great to get your message across, but also shows you are a commander. You don't eschew a fight but strike back. Take courses and work on your body language and tone of voice so that you radiate calmness and dominance.

Let's look at a good illustration of how not to act. Ed Muskie was the favorite to clinch the 1968 nomination of the US Democratic Party. His momentum, however, collapsed before the primary ballot when a slandering letter was disseminated. The newspaper that published the letter also attacked the character of Muskie's wife. Muskie conveyed the press and made an emotional defense of his wife. It is said he broke down and cried during the press conference. It shattered his image as a calm and reasoned person. The people don't want leaders who break down. And so Muskie's candidacy was destroyed.

Subconscious parts of our brain evaluate all relations based on hierarchy. The tone of speech, the way people move, touch, or look at each other, all shape our perception of a person's rank. For example, mammals (including humans) experience individuals with deep voices as more dominant. Among males, higher levels of testosterone are associated with lower-pitched tones. This essential hormone affects our social behavior.

In the past, women used to speak with higher pitches. That can be studied in audio fragments from the early 20th century. A high pitch was culturally deemed feminine and attractive. Since then, the position of women in society has changed. As women entered politics and business en masse, power structures evolved. And so did their voice: women on average have a much deeper voice than a century before.

Margaret Thatcher—a most successful politician—employed a personal coach to train her voice. This training enabled her to lower the pitch of her voice at will. Her deep voice influenced the public, who subconsciously deemed her more authoritative because of it. She hacked in this way the brain of those listening.

(3) Competence

Next to trust and leadership, you also have to demonstrate skill and intelligence. After all, you will have to manage the largest and most important administration of your country. It is wise to first acquire some experience as a governor of a province or a minister of the government. This allows you to claim expertise and cite your past accomplishments.

Also cycle with your staff through any popular topic or subject that could be thrown at you till you master them. Pretend your answers are genuine and improvised, but rehearse them beforehand, especially for debates. A prepared individual is worth two; an unprepared one sounds foolish.

Gary Johnson was the candidate of the Libertarian Party in the 2016 US election. When questioned on the events in Aleppo (Syria), he sounded puzzled. Gary Johnson had no clue where Aleppo was located or what had happened there. He showed zero interest in and understanding of the Syrian Civil War. ''What is Aleppo?'' remained the only contribution of the confused Gary Johnson to the 2016 campaign. Voters are on the lookout for such incompetence and will punish these candidates.

A positive example to follow is Bart De Wever, the Belgian politician who gathered the most votes in recent elections. He became in 2004 the leader of a small party called the N-VA. De Wever participated back then in a popular and recurrent Flemish television quiz. He kept winning the quiz and made it to the grand finals of the season. Though his participation gave him a lot of free publicity as well, it above all served to prove his knowledge and ability. In the 2010 election, the N-VA directed by De Wever skyrocketed from a couple of percentage points to close to 30% of the vote.

Trust, leadership, and competence; these characteristics matter the most. You have to prove that you possess all three or, at least, project the image you have all three. Do good things and have others talk about it. Get the word out and have others endorse you. Never let an opponent get away with the claim that you are untrustworthy, or a coward, or incompetent. Always look to undermine your opponent's claims at those qualities.

But who are you for real

The qualities mentioned above are the foremost traits you pretend to possess because the population expects them from a president. They are not the only traits that will help you to win the presidency. When looking inside, a successful candidate will need to nurture different characteristics as well.

You need ambition, which compels you to set yourself the highest possible goal. You need discipline, to carry out the unpleasant things necessary to reach the goal and reap its reward. And you need resilience and self-confidence, to withstand the quirks of fate and the criticism you will endure.

However, to the outside, it is better to hide your aspiration to the highest position. Never state your real intention. Voters don't like shrewd, ambitious, and ruthless politicians, even though all those traits are required to win the presidential race. Therefore, pretend to have been compelled to run for president. Mask your desire for power and wish to govern the country. Tell them instead you run for office because you want to defend the common people. You want to protect them from injustice, from impending danger, from the entrenched minority, and from your rivals' incompetence and dishonesty. This election isn't about you, but where the nation is heading. Narrate them a wonderful story about how citizens implored you to run or how you didn't want, but the country called you. Somehow, it works every time.

Two times President of Chile Michelle Bachelet in her second run declared she at first did not seek re-election, but had responded to the call of citizens. She launched her campaign with an astute video showing the faces of the people who urged her to run. Therein, one could see individuals acclaiming and praising her after meeting her face-to-face to discuss the issues on their minds. This video was disseminated online and on social networks. And in this manner, she proved that (1) she had been asked to participate and (2) was close to the people.

More than twenty years earlier, Ross Perot, as an independent candidate in the US election, had acted likewise. During an appearance on a TV show, the host asked Perot if he would run for President of the United States. Perot announced first that he did not want to run, feigning modesty and disinterest. Then he added that he would consider it if ordinary people signed petitions and helped him achieve ballot access in all 50 states. Soon after that, with the help of a phone bank at his office, thousands of citizens turned this into reality.

The incumbent President of Iceland in 2012, Ólafur Ragnar Grímsson, professed he did not wish to seek re-election. Yet later, he declared he would run for another term, because he received a petition of over 30,000 voters in favor of his candidacy. He said:

''Under normal circumstances, I would have come to a different conclusion, but [...] the Icelanders requested that I continue.'' He didn't appear shrewd or ambitious to the Icelandic people. And such well-acted deception gained him five times the presidency.

A word on empathy. You will need to promise popular policies. You will investigate what people like through surveys and physical meetings. A gathering is not as efficient as online surveys to collect lots of data, but allows you to feel the beat live. Although physical presence can ease understanding of what is on people's minds, don't let a single person impress you. An anecdote is not statistics. Furthermore, your campaign team can later use a couple of well-taken videos or photos from the event. You can so profit by making the public believe you are doing this all the time. It will prove that you have compassion, even though, in reality, you are only using empathy to achieve your own goals.

A president should never be humble inside. No matter how intelligent you are, how many policies you propose, or how many people you have helped, you will always receive a lot of criticisms. Presidents are often beaten up by the press, opponents, and even allies. Antisthenes, an ancient Greek philosopher, already noted that "It is a royal privilege to do good and be ill spoken of."

Ego is the only way to endure it. A bit of narcissism helps you survive it all. Maintain this mindset: "Love yourself, no matter what." Inside your head, you are doing great things for the country, you are a winner, and the opponents are envious losers. And remember that outward humility is either shyness or well-executed acting. All presidents are or were total narcissists because that is what's needed to attain the highest position.

How to deal with baggage

You might have some baggage, which is stuff you said or did in the past that can now be wielded to place your person in an unfavorable light. If your opponent has any sense of campaign tactics, he will—like you—have done opposition research. You have to assume that unsavory details from your past are dug up and brought to light.

Three approaches are possible to deal with such cases. Either you draft beforehand an answer that you will use in case the incident is reported. You will not be caught off-guard, and it will allow you to execute a prepared counterattack. Or you could explain the case before the opponent gets to it. Info revealed by yourself is less damaging than your opponent exposing it to the voters. The last alternative is to refuse to admit or offer apologies and counterattack in strength. On the bright side, this will give you some free airtime because the media will talk about you.

Never apologize, though, for it will lose you authority. Either you made a huge mistake, and you are out anyway. Or it was only a minor mistake, and you will look weak apologizing. For many people, it won't be clear if what you said was a big deal or not. If you apologize extensively, it will look like you did something seriously wrong or that you are a submissive person. Instead, you should laugh the accusation away as a small thing and so downplay it.

A good case study comes from Bill Clinton, who immediately admitted when he was questioned on using drugs: ''When I was in England I experimented with marijuana a time or two, and I didn't like it. I didn't inhale it, and never tried it again.'' That was a solid answer because (1) he reveals damaging info before his opponents can exploit it, (2) he doesn't lie, (3) he downplays it, and (4) his response is funny (''I didn't inhale''). Imagine he would have denied it, but then would have been confronted with contrary evidence. It would have damaged or even destroyed his reputation by giving food for his rival's campaign. Instead, Clinton's preemptive avowal left his opponents with no good avenues to create a scandal since it was already 'old-news'.

Dominate political debates

Political debates are a prime time to shine, and a great moment to cast a negative light over your rivals. In presidential systems, it is about the individual more so than the party's program. Debates will further accentuate your personality. Nuanced policy proposals are hard to describe in detail during a discussion, in particular when many candidates are on stage. Exchanges happen through short soundbites, where each contestant tries to place his or her punchline. The media will summarize the clash in a 30sec fragment. Discussion among participants does not yield new insights. You won't persuade people with thought-out arguments in such contests because substance matters less than style. The setup of political debates does not generate a clash of logic (logos), but rather a clash of personalities (ethos).

Intelligent persons will have read your program anyway. They understand this debate is only for the show, almost like a play. After all, don't the candidates stand on a stage? So when debating, it is the less informed and less smart individuals you need to convince. Your goal is to appeal to their emotions and reveal your personality within that short time-frame. Show dominance and the values for which you stand. Don't waste time on policy details since the public doesn't care. You will bore them, especially when mentioning amounts like the cost of programs. If you are unknown or have low name recognition, your objective is to make a splash on stage. And, in general, you should aim to send the other contenders limping back home. How to achieve this?

First, an example on how you shouldn't act. In the 1988 United States presidential election, a debate was held between George H.W. Bush and Michael Dukakis. The moderator opened the talk by asking Dukakis if he still would support abolishing the death penalty if his wife was raped and murdered. Dukakis seemed unperturbed by this provocative question. Without any trace of emotion, he answered back with a lecturing tone that he had opposed the death penalty during all of his life. Dukakis proceeded to try to support his view by mentioning some statistics. He sounded like a professor in front of pupils. What a terrible mistake he made. Presidential debates are not decided by reasoned arguments but by passion and values. One cannot imagine a worse answer.

What should he have done instead? You don't have to answer obediently like Dukakis. A debate is anyhow not about reason, but about showing who you are and what you stand for. That doesn't always require a straight-up answer. Dukakis should immediately have called out the journalist for this disgusting question. It would have shown that he was passionate, loved his wife, and wouldn't let a journalist get away with such repugnant questioning. Don't let yourself be trampled over. Lasting leaders are not at the mercy of journalists. They take control of the discussion. Dukakis should have continued with a counterattack on the sensationalist media that obviously favored his opponent. Or he could have argued that the gluttonous media pursues incessant division, and is to blame for the growing polarization (and also many other things). Next, he could declare he would make a stand against this. Dukakis could further have mentioned that his wife was watching, and his children to. He could so appeal to the empathy of the audience; the public would understand that Dukakis was like one of them. It was the ideal question to answer, because he could have applied so many strategies described within this book. But replying with some statistics on the topic, that was shooting oneself in the foot.

It is Nature's law that people prefer to have dominant and authoritative individuals in charge. Debates are meant to prove superiority over other candidates. Demonstrate you are a leader and your rivals are unfit for command. Be dominant, establish your supremacy, show you are not afraid. The audience expects a bit of aggressiveness and assertiveness from a true leader. So, don't hesitate to interrupt your opponents, although don't do it too often and don't be too rude.

An excellent example is the presidential debate in 2012 between the incumbent Nicolas Sarkozy and his contestant, François Hollande. Hollande, the candidate of the French socialist party, had a reputation of a soft person and consensus builder. Yet he adapted his style and performed very well in the debate against Sarkozy. Here is an extract:

Sarkozy: ''That is maybe what makes us different. And ...''

Hollande: "[interrupts] Yes, that's probably what makes us different."

Sarkozy: "And as such, if you will allow me to finish …"

Hollande: "… if you haven't finished, I'll let you."

What can be gleaned from this altercation? Although Hollande keeps a mask of politeness, he shows assertiveness. He does so by firstly interrupting his opponent, and secondly, by letting (almost as if he was allowing) him to finish. It leaves no doubt who is in charge, as Hollande implies he authorizes Sarkozy to complete his statement. The exchange was favorable for Hollande, who went on to win the close election. In an almost identical manner, President Obama interrupted his opponent in 2012. Then he said to Romney: "Please proceed."

Such an intervention in your rival's speech can unnerve them and will lead them to mistakes. You should try to cause the collapse of the other by throwing him or her off-balance.

What happens if you are interrupted? You have to learn to react well. Train with someone from your staff. That person's role is to put you off balance by interrupting you. You have to become accustomed to interruption. After some practice, you will develop 3-4 lines you can retort with. Also, your tone and style should adapt to refute any such attempt. Don't let your rivals break into your speech at will; you are the leader after all.

As illustration, in the GOP primary, Jeb Bush was deemed the favorite at the start. He did flop hard in the debates though. Bush was repeatedly criticized for being a puppet and low energy. These are classical attacks based on ethos (someone's character) and not on logos or pathos. After Jeb Bush interrupted him, Donald Trump flatly told Jeb to be quiet. Jeb Bush blushed and then remained silent, revealing himself to be inferior and subordinate. Trump is a strong debater and came out very well in the primary debates. He would not hesitate to disrespect opponents (''low energy guy'', ''you are surely such a tough guy''), thereby establishing his dominance.

Understand that a promising campaign following the advice of previous chapters is not sufficient. You can still fail if you falter on stage in front of the crowds. If you don't speak up during the contest, you won't succeed. If you don't show yourself a calm, confident leader, people won't vote for you. If you let other candidates steal the show and walk you over, you will seem like a loser.

Don't be too aggressive, though, as had been Ségolène Royal in her debate against the same Sarkozy in 2007. When the topic of disabled children came up, Ségolène Royal, started raging against the immorality of Nicolas Sarkozy to such extent that it looked overdone. Sarkozy coolly replied that Royal had ''lost her nerve'' and that one has to ''remain calm as a president.'' His lecturing her about keeping her calm was the climax of the evening. With that exchange, Sarkozy won according to all polls the debate. A week later, he became with 53% of the vote, the new President of France.

The audience experiences calm persons as more confident, more dominant, and in control. If you lose your calm in a debate over some policy proposal, how will you react when Pearl Harbor is bombed? So it is a balancing act: you have to appeal to their emotions, yet remain calm yourself. Assert dominance, but don't show arrogance or excessive rudeness. And remember that debates are foremost about personality revealed.

When you are attacked in a debate, strike back. No challenge is one too many for you. There are many suitable ways to react to an attack.

The first technique, as in Judo, is to use the momentum of the assault against the attacker. When donors of the Republican Party booed him, Donald Trump used this as proof his opponents were puppets in the hands of donors. He thus demonstrated that he only was the true defender of the common people. Ross Perot, the independent candidate in the US 1992 election, was criticized for his lack of governmental experience. When asked to respond to his detractors' claims, he remarked: ''Well, they've got a point. I don't have any experience running up a $4 trillion debt.'' And so he struck back with one of his main policy proposals, namely the reduction of the deficit and national debt which endangered American prosperity.

The second method is a diversion to deflect whatever they are throwing at you. If you see a vulnerability in the attack, focus your response on that detail. If you can catch the opponent in a lie or inaccuracy, the entire attack can collapse even though the rest was left unanswered. That will draw attention away from the core of the criticism. You can achieve this either by name-calling your enemy and drawing attention to his or her vulnerabilities. Or you could answer with humor, which makes people forget the attack. A humorous reply will make you likable and generate trust. When Carter attacked Reagan during the presidential debate in 1980, with a long monologue on Medicare, Reagan simply responded with ''There you go again.'' Being funny is an asset you can exploit to your advantage. So train your wit and keep some jokes in your pocket, as did the two times President of the United States Ronald Reagan, who was a master at this. When he was challenged on his advanced age during the 1984 debate, he retorted: "I will not make age an issue in this campaign. I will not exploit, for political purposes, my opponent's youth and inexperience." This single line changed the debate and the election. Even his opponent, Walter Mondale, was laughing on television with the joke of his opponent. When debating taxes, Mondale repeatedly attacked Reagan for lowering taxes and hammered on higher taxes. Ronald Reagan next said to Walter Mondale: "I'd say you were taxing my patience, but it would just give you another idea."

The third way of routing an attack is to take a step back. Face attacks without going into your opponent's game. Don't allow them to set the overall frame and don't get pushed in a defensive position. In France in 1974, a debate between the socialist candidate François Mitterrand and incumbent Giscard d'Estaing was held before the second turn vote. Mitterrand attacked his opponent for favoring the very few. Why didn't the president share the fruits of labor broadly? Mitterrand wanted not only economic but also social progress. Although d'Estaing could have justified his policies, this would have been a mistake. If you directly defend yourself, you let the enemy dictate the tempo and set the narrative. In this case, it would have meant that d'Estaing tacitly agreed with the initial statement that he was a heartless president. Better is to step outside of the framing of your opponent and retake the initiative. What did d'Estaing respond to that? He said: "Mr. Mitterrand, you don't have a monopoly on the heart. It's a hurtful statement to others. I, too, have a heart." And so he turned the tables on Mitterrand.

Many opponents or journalists will try to trick you with such loaded questions or insinuations. Take the classic example "Have you stopped beating your wife?'' It implies or assumes that you beat your wife in the first place. Don't let your opponent establish this assumption as truth. Instead, point out the inherent flaw in the premise behind it. In the French debate in 2012, Nicolas Sarkozy said against his opponent, ''What you might not know, Mr. Hollande, is …'' François Hollande promptly interrupted and said, ''You don't know what I know. You are not my teacher.'' That is how he sidestepped Sarkozy's ambush. The failed attack made Nicolas Sarkozy look arrogant and a know-it-all. By disrupting his opponent's speech and putting Sarkozy back in his place, Hollande furthermore established he was in charge.

Hone your debating skills and train with your advisers. Practice these three methods so that you are prepared to face any attack.

In such verbal jousting, you have to strike when your opponent shows a weakness. In the French debate in 2017 between the two candidates in the second round of the election, Emmanuel Macron faced Marine Le Pen. The discussion was a resounding victory for Macron. Mrs. Le Pen didn't master specific issues. She mixed up a case involving a major company producing phones with another case involving an industrial equipment producer. Macron didn't fail to point out factual errors: ''It is sad for you, because you show your unpreparedness to our fellow citizens. You won't last long if you are mixing up the two [cases].'' And so he undermined the perception of her skill. A newspaper described the discussion as a 2.5-hour long shipwreck for Le Pen. In a culminating exchange thereafter, Macron seized the opportunity and demolished her: ''Ce que vous proposer, comme d'habitude, c'est de la poudre de perlimpinpin.'' (What you propose, as always, is magic voodoo power.) Le Pen could not formulate a reply and broke down. Through his words and actions, Macron demonstrated that Le Pen was dishonest, had no plan, and was unfit for command. In this fashion, Macron cemented his lead and outperformed all polls in the second round.

In a debate, you have to be like a tiger: when your prey makes a misstep and is vulnerable, jump on it, and aim for the throat. Don't let an opponent escape unharmed from a blunder.

Conversely, you cannot afford any slack when debating, for, in one moment, you can lose all your chances. Make sure to be good on stage. Hire debating experts, review past debates, and train, train, train. A prepared person is worth two.

In history, a considerable number of candidates, who at first had good shots at winning, were destroyed in debates by an adversary. Marco Rubio was, at first, a favorite in the 2016 US Republican primary. According to all polls, he was a front-runner. In a subsequent debate, however, he made an error and sounded scripted. Another candidate, Chris Christie, jumped on it and pounded with all might accusing Rubio of lacking experience and being a hollow Washington politician. Marco Rubio couldn't formulate a good answer and kept repeating the same scripted 25 seconds speech, like a robot. He humiliated himself. His image was shattered after this fiasco, and he suspended his campaign.

In summary of this chapter, pay attention to your character traits. You have to work just as hard on your image and behavior, as on your campaign content and strategy. Play your role, for you are an actor/actress.

Chapter 12
Pretend you are one of them

All the world's a stage,
And all the men and women merely players
— *William Shakespeare*

How well-thought and intelligent your policy proposals are doesn't matter. The electorate isn't interested in those. Emotions (pathos) and who you are (ethos) decide elections. I have already touched upon pathos, mostly in the Part I and II. On ethos's side, you must not appear arrogant. Regardless of the exact rules of the presidential elections, you will need to convince the majority that you defend the common man. That you will FIGHT for them. You are not an elitist but one of them.

Give people hope as even the most cynical wants to believe in someone, as wrote Quintus Tullius 2000 years ago. Persuade them that you are one of them, that you stand at their side, and will make the country a better place. They will follow and support you—at least until after the election, when you will inevitably let them down.

You are close to the people

The common man will punish any candidate that appears to be out of touch. So at all times, you will behave like them, talk like them, joke like them, appeal to them. It is useful to know by heart the price of eggs or milk, to show off when you are interrogated. Too many candidates have, in the past, been caught off guard by such mundane questions. Signal to the voter that you as well shop for groceries, change diapers of newborns, sit in traffic jams, and support some sports team.

A study case is the 1992 town hall debate between Bush and Clinton, where a member of the audience asked: ''How has the national debt personally affected each of your lives? And if it hasn't, how can you honestly find a cure for the economic problems of the common people if you have no experience in what's ailing them?''

George Bush didn't understand the question and stumbled upon his words. To be fair, the problem was ill-posed. Most people can't tell how the national debt is impacting them. And national debt doesn't necessarily relate to layoffs. The woman was talking about the national debt when she, in reality, meant the economic crisis. Yet nothing excuses Bush's weak response. He should have heeded Mc Namara's advice: ''Never answer the question that is asked of you. Answer the question that you wish had been asked of you.''

Bill Clinton, in contrast, reacted well. He stated that as a governor, he met all the people of his state that been laid off, that he knew all their names. That was blatant lying—it is not possible to know the names of all those laid off—, but that doesn't matter. What matters is that he showed concern. He met bankrupted businesses, he met laid off people, and he understood the ordinary people. Clinton assured that he had been in the first line, next to them, in the face of the economic downturn. That was the right attitude to display because that is someone voters can connect to.

Voters need to be able to identify with you, which is why you need to be upfront and employ plain language instead of lawyer-speak. Otherwise, people will be distrustful of your good intentions.

But words alone don't always suffice. You have to, furthermore, signal through your deeds that you are the defender of the people. For illustration, Giscard d'Estaing, President of France for seven years, would regularly dine with a random French family. The head of the state would at the table ask about daily life. And he fraternized with the head of the family. The hosts would then appear on television and recount the dinner. It was a great publicity stunt, since these simple and friendly dinners proved he was close to the people.

Don't be condescending

No one likes a know-it-all. (Or at least, this is how dumb persons might perceive you.) Voters will regard those who lecture them as arrogant. Outward arrogance is a cardinal sin when striving for the highest office. Even if you are more gifted, don't appear wiser than the people since voters distrust cleverness and intellectuals. Many elections were lost by merely forgetting this simple rule. Let's look at good and bad cases from history.

A recent incident illustrating how one should not act comes from the US 2016 presidential campaign. Hillary Clinton defied this advice, much to her later chagrin. That happened not even during a debate where she had to improvise but during a prepared speech. It was an unforced error. She named Trump supporters ''a basket of deplorables.'' Such condescension should never be revealed; you won't win by lamenting about half of the population. Clinton later admitted her gaffe in her book 'What Happened'.

On the other side of the coin, if your opponent makes such assertions, hammer on his or her mistake. Trump's campaign took advantage of Hillary's blunder during rallies, debates, and advertisements. He, for example, declared at a rally: ''While my opponent slanders you as deplorable and irredeemable, I call you hardworking American patriots who love your country.'' His team proceeded with sales of T-shirts and other goodies featuring the phrase. That is the correct way of campaigning. You too should pretend to defend hardworking ordinary citizens and rail against your elitist opponent.

Don't make condescending comments even if you are in a private meeting, as Mitt Romney, a candidate to the US presidency in 2012 discovered. Romney was polling quite well. Although he delivered a solid debate performance versus Obama, he eventually lost the election. How did this happen? Romney remarked on a private fundraiser meeting that ''there are 47 percent [of the voters], who are dependent upon government, who believe that they are victims, who believe that they are entitled to health care, to food, to housing, to you-name-it. These are people who pay no income tax. And they will vote for Obama no matter what.'' A video of this meeting was subsequently leaked, and Romney couldn't deny his statement. That was the campaign losing moment for Romney. His ''47 percent'' comment revealed him as an out-of-touch rich guy who held disdain for the common man. On Election Day, Romney only gathered 47% of the vote. It is fine to bash a minority. It is even an excellent strategy to achieve the presidency, as outlined in a previous chapter. But you can't criticize 47%. You can't say they are entitled losers. You have to appeal to broad swathes of the electorate.

Emmanuel Macron, the current President of France, also made a series of 'gaffes'. That was, however, after he already won the elections. His popularity ratings nevertheless took a hit. His remarks still deserve mention because they will affect his re-election chances in 2022. For example, when meeting unemployed youth, he asserted: ''I'll cross the street, I'll find you a job.'' That dramatically downplayed the difficulty of finding a job in a country where one young adult out of four was unemployed.

Furthermore, he complained in public about ''the stubborn Gaul [=French] resisting change.'' Criticizing your own people in such a demeaning way is a blunder you should avoid at all costs. Never appear obnoxious, as Macron did, and always feign humility. Recall that humbleness is either shyness or a well-executed PR stunt.

Positive examples you should emulate are ''I am your voice'' and paying lip service to the people. Donald Trump, for instance, stated ''What truly matters is not which party controls our government, but whether our government is controlled by the people. January 20th 2017, will be remembered as the day the people became the rulers of this nation again. Those forgotten will no longer be forgotten.'' And Obama, during his debate with Romney, promised: ''I will fight every single day on behalf of the American people in the middle class and all those that are striving to get in the middle class.''

*

In summary of this chapter, when striving for the presidency, pretend you will stand for the average person. Pose as their champion. Do this through words and acts. And above all, avoid any missteps. This book allows you to learn in a short time from others' mistakes. Your political career is too short to make them all yourself.

What's next

Screw it, let's do it!
— Richard Branson

The electorate keeps hoping and praying for a Messiah, a strong president that will slice the Gordian knot. They wish for a chief that cleanses the corruption. You are that person. If you are a gifted individual aspiring greatness, then pursue politics and become president. Winning the presidential election is the highest art of human understanding, empathy, and emotional intelligence. You can run for office. You can be Head of State, provided you follow the advice and templates set out in this book. Don't do things that cause you to feel good, do stuff that works. Never forget that voters are tools that you employ to achieve your goals.

You need to set out a strategy on how you will win. What are your key issues, how will you make a splash, on whom will you concentrate the blame? What will your slogan be? Develop your plan and implement it with the help of your team. How will you counter the attack of your enemies? And remember: there can be only one winner. This is not a parliamentary democracy where you might need to ally other parties after the elections. You won't need to share power others. Other contestants are hence enemies. They are obstacles in your path that need to be trampled and leveled.

What if you now have snatched victory and are president? Congratulations. Now call to unity. That is kind of convenient as you will be the boss at present, behind whom they need to rally.

As president, you are the legitimate head of state, head of the executive. You are the representative of the entire nation.

On the other hand, some bad losers will still resent you. The opposition will say you clearly are a partisan political option and do not represent the whole nation. Yet you are president now. Hence, walk over them regardless if you won with a 0.1 or 50 point lead. Escalate the conflict against the legislative branch if they seek to block your projects. There is no need to dialogue with the opposing side since the people chose you, and therefore you have a direct mandate from them. You, by definition, reflect and represent the popular will.

You will bring strong and stable leadership to the nation. At least for a while. Once you are in office, you will, of course, be burdened by the shackles of reality. The power you now possess might be hopelessly insufficient to meet the expectations you have generated. Down the road, you will have to face an angry mob looking for a scapegoat.

Thereafter, write your memoirs. That will allow you to shape the opinion future generations will hold of you. Churchill, Reagan, Chirac all wrote memoirs and became more popular and respected over time. For perception is reality.

Acknowledgments

I am happy to acknowledge the help of Marius Petitzon, my brother, who went through multiple drafts. His constructive suggestions and detailed comments were essential for making this a better book. I am grateful for his support.

Thank you, as well, to all those giants that have come before me.

Copyright

FIRST EDITION

ISBN 9798606757770

Credits

The cover is based on the picture "Lawn in front of the White House, Washington, DC," by Daniel Schwen, 2008. Accessed on January 20, 2020, Wiki/White_House_lawn.jpg is licensed under the Creative Commons Attribution-Share Alike 2.5 Generic.

Index

A

advertising
    A/B testing
    advertising industry
    Daisy ad
    marketing departments
    negative advertisements
    targeted ads
Affordable Care Act
Ahmadinejad, Mahmoud
Allende, Salvador
America First
Arab Spring

B

Bachelet, Michelle
bandwagon effect
basket of deplorables
battleground state
Bayesian statistics
behavior of the masses
Berlusconi, Silvio
Bolsonaro, Jair
Brexit
    Vote Leave
budget deficit
Bush vs. Gore

D

Hippies
Hollande, François

I
Icesave Case
immigration
    Hispanics immigrants
    Italian immigration
    middle-eastern
    Venezuelan refugees
incentive
intellectual
Intergovernmental Panel on Climate Change (IPCC)
International Monetary Fund (IMF)
invasions of Eastern-Europe
Iohannis, Klaus

J
Jae-in, Moon
Jews
Johnson, Garry
Johnson, Lyndon B.
Jospin, Lionel

K
Kennedy, John F.
Kerry, John

L

Schwarzenegger, Arnold

Sirisena, Maithripala

sophist

Spencer, Oswald

student debt, cancellation of

T

Tamils

Tancredo, Tom

tariff

tax, wealth

taxes

taxpayer money

terrorism

Thatcher, Margaret

The Limits to Growth (1972)

Trump, Donald J.

Tsipras, Alexis

V

Van Der Bellen, Alexander

voter turnout

voting mechanism

    electoral college

    first-past-the-post

    one-turn vote (plurality)

    proportional

    two-turn vote

W

Z